# Farm Fresh Southern Cooking

*Straight from the Garden to Your Dinner Table*

## TAMMY ALGOOD

**Thomas Nelson**
*Since 1798*

NASHVILLE   DALLAS   MEXICO CITY   RIO DE JANEIRO

Published in Nashville, Tennessee, by Thomas Nelson. Thomas Nelson
is a registered trademark of Thomas Nelson, Inc.

Photography by Ron Manville

Food styling by Teresa Blackburn

Images on the following pages are from Thinkstockphotos.com: 49, 69, 87, 89, 107, 173,
185, 196

Thomas Nelson, Inc., titles may be purchased in bulk for educational,
business, fund-raising, or sales promotional use. For information, please
e-mail SpecialMarkets@ThomasNelson.com.

**Library of Congress Cataloging-in-Publication Data**

Algood, Tammy.
  Farm fresh Southern cooking : straight from the garden to your dinner table / Tammy Algood.
      p. cm.
  ISBN 978-1-4016-0158-4
  1. Cooking, American—Southern style. 2. Cooking (Vegetables) 3. Cooking (Fruit)
4. Cookbooks. I. Title.
  TX715.2.S68A39 2012
  641.5975—dc23                                                    2011041377

*Printed in the United States of America*

12 13 14 15 16 QG 6 5 4 3 2 1

To my husband, George, who taught me how to love life richly, deeply, and completely.

# Contents

# Introduction

*I* think I have always been a farm girl even though I have never lived on an actual farm. There is something about the entire lifestyle that I can identify with and that I admire and adore. It's that depth of appreciation for farmers and agriculture that has greatly influenced my food choices throughout my whole life.

Locally grown, seasonal fresh foods that are sold straight from the producer to the consumer are more than just a passing fad. These unprocessed, beautifully natural

foods have become a way of life not just for me, but for countless others in this country and beyond our borders. To that, I say, "Glory!"

In my two decades of promoting foods produced from your own community backyards, I've noticed something interesting. The challenge for a lot of people is how to locate local. Well, believe it or not, it's easier than you may think and doesn't involve endless trips all over the Southern countryside.

Start with the farmers' market that is in or around your town. I promise you there is one, whether you know about it or not. The easiest way to find it is to go online at the Department of Agriculture in your own state. You'll be surprised at the treasures you'll find on their websites. Not only do they have listings of community farmers' markets, but of individual growers and producers as well. Most have local farm locator maps, divided by county or parish, making it a cinch to find those that are close to your kitchen.

You'll also find produce availability charts to direct you through the local season wherever you live, in the South or not. Use it through the entire year as your guide to where to find the freshest food at your fingertips. You will quickly see that it is an invaluable resource, so go ahead and bookmark the site as one of your favorites, because it soon will be just that.

Don't stop there. Pay close attention to your local newspaper. If you don't

subscribe to one, make it a point to do so today. It is an "in the hand" connection to your community and a wonderfully wise investment. You'll see loads of advertisements from food producers of every kind within the pages. Find them! Get to know the people around you.

Last, make it a point to shop for local foods as you travel. It's easy to forget that neighboring states—north, south, east, or west—have growing conditions that differ vastly from your own. Those other areas can be sources of unique food items that make routine meals tastier and a lot more interesting. Frequent welcome centers along interstates, and stand in front of those overwhelming tourist brochure racks. Hidden among the slots are gems of local food outlets including everything from ice cream parlors to goat cheese farms.

My hope is that this cookbook will inspire you to cook fresh and enjoy the bounty we routinely receive from our precious land. Annually, we are given incredible food gifts that sometimes subtly and other times dramatically shift and change in texture and flavor as the days move from long to short. The earth is nature's grocery store and quite honestly, the finest food market I've ever seen. Make it your regular stop and you'll be amazed at the difference it makes when that food—especially when it's close to home—is placed on your breakfast, lunch, and dinner table.

There is nothing better than knowing who grew or made the foods you enjoy daily. It will change your recipes, your enjoyment of food shopping, and your entire attitude about which foods are just good and which ones are great. So go ahead and get started . . . local is calling!

# Appetizers

Crawfish-Stuffed Mushrooms

Pocketbook Pleaser Sweet Potato Chutney

Green Tomato Salsa

Not for Wimps Shrimp Dip

Tomato and Double Cheese Fondue

Caramelized Onion and Mushroom Triangles

Coconut Fried Shrimp and Florida Citrus Dip

Spring Green Spread

Cheese-Filled Banana Peppers

Pea-Picking Salsa

Spiced Peach Chutney

Lazy Afternoon Fruit Salsa

Party Time Rhubarb Chutney

Pickled Figs

Roasted Eggplant Dip

Great Grapes

Spring Celebration Cucumber Plates

Kernels of Wisdom Salsa

Time-Honored Cheese Crackers

Golden Brown Goat Cheese Medallions

Spring Street Bean Spread

Good to the Core Apple Chutney

Roasted Bacon Pecans

"Where's the Party?" Broccoli Dip

Fresh Peach Salsa

This is an elegant appetizer that is perfect for a patio party. I love the interest that crawfish adds to this dish, and it's spiced just right to please both those who love heat and those who shy away from it.

❧

Preheat the oven to 350°F. Lightly grease a 13 x 9-inch baking dish. Place the mushroom caps in the baking dish and set aside.

In a large skillet over medium heat, melt 3 tablespoons of the butter. Add the onions, celery, peppers, and parsley. Sauté 4 minutes and stir in the thyme, salt, pepper, hot sauce, crawfish, and breadcrumbs.

Remove from the heat and carefully spoon the crawfish mixture into the mushroom caps. Melt the remaining butter and drizzle over the tops. Sprinkle lightly with paprika. Bake 12 to 15 minutes. Serve warm.

* Save the mushrooms stems for sprinkling on a salad.

# Crawfish-Stuffed Mushrooms

**Makes 8 to 10 servings**

20 large fresh mushrooms, cleaned and stems removed*

6 tablespoons unsalted butter, divided

1/2 cup diced onions

1/4 cup diced celery

1/4 cup diced green bell peppers

1 tablespoon chopped fresh parsley

1/2 teaspoon dried ground thyme

1/2 teaspoon salt

1/4 teaspoon black pepper

1/2 teaspoon hot sauce

1 pound crawfish tails, cooked, peeled, and chopped

1 cup seasoned dry breadcrumbs

Paprika

# Pocketbook Pleaser Sweet Potato Chutney

**Makes 2½ cups**

1 sweet potato, cooked, peeled, and diced

1 Golden Delicious apple, cored and diced

3 green onions, chopped

3 tablespoons chopped fresh parsley

1 celery stalk, chopped

2 tablespoons cider vinegar

2 tablespoons thawed frozen apple juice concentrate

2 tablespoons minced crystallized ginger

1/4 teaspoon black pepper

1/8 teaspoon kosher salt

This chutney is so good and looks terrific. It makes a great appetizer when served with nice crackers and slices of smoked Cheddar. I also serve a dollop on cooked pork, where both shine. It will pull even the most simply roasted meat into the fancy category. You won't be able to get enough! Use the leftover apple juice concentrate to make a pitcher of juice.

Place the potatoes, apples, onions, parsley, and celery in a serving bowl and gently toss to combine. In a small bowl, whisk together the vinegar, apple juice concentrate, ginger, pepper, and salt. Drizzle over the sweet potato mixture and gently toss to evenly coat.

Cover and refrigerate at least 2 hours before serving. Toss again before serving.

**Note:** Leftovers keep up to a week in the refrigerator.

It's time to go color-blind with salsa, because not all salsa has to be red. This one is excellent with low-salt or homemade tortilla chips. But don't leave it there. It can also be a garnish on grilled chicken, pork, or fish.

જી

In a large bowl, gently combine the tomatoes, garlic, onions, cilantro, juice, peppers, salt, and pepper. Cover and refrigerate at least 2 hours.

Bring to room temperature before serving.

# Green Tomato Salsa

Makes 2½ cups

1 pound green tomatoes, cut in large dice
3 garlic cloves, minced
4 green onions, sliced
¼ cup chopped cilantro
1 tablespoon lime juice
2 jalapeño peppers, seeded and minced
½ teaspoon kosher salt
¼ teaspoon black pepper

A thin chip or cracker simply cannot hold up to this chunky dip. Use scoop-type chips or crostini, and serve with a crisp white wine for an elegant appetizer your guests will love.

જી

In the bowl of an electric mixer, combine the cheese, mayonnaise, pepper liquid, and mustard on low speed. Fold in the shrimp, celery, onions, and peppers. Transfer to a serving bowl. Cover and refrigerate at least 1 hour before serving.

Serve chilled with hefty chips or crackers.

# Not for Wimps Shrimp Dip

Makes 5 cups

2 (8-ounce) packages cream cheese, softened
½ cup mayonnaise
½ teaspoon pickled jalapeño pepper liquid
1 tablespoon prepared mustard
1½ pounds cooked salad shrimp
3 celery stalks, finely chopped
6 green onions, chopped
2 tablespoons chopped pickled jalapeño peppers

Cheeses with an almost nutty flavor are paired with sweet, ripe tomatoes. The creamy, warm mixture is excellent to use for dunking chunks of crusty bread or even roasted meats.

❧

Place the tomatoes and garlic in a fondue pot set on medium heat. Cook until soft, about 4 minutes, stirring constantly. Add half of the juice and cook 3 minutes longer. Stir in the cheeses.

In a separate bowl, combine the cornstarch, remaining juice, and cream. Stir until smooth and add to the tomato mixture. When the cheese is melted, season with the pepper and oregano. Serve warm with bread cubes.

# Tomato and Double Cheese Fondue

**Makes 8 servings**

10 plum tomatoes, peeled, seeded, and chopped

2 garlic cloves, minced

$1/2$ cup tomato juice, divided

10 ounces grated Gruyère cheese

10 ounces grated Emmentaler cheese

4 teaspoons cornstarch

1 tablespoon cream

$1/4$ teaspoon white pepper

$1/8$ teaspoon dried oregano

Bread cubes for dipping

# Caramelized Onion and Mushroom Triangles

**Makes 12 servings**

1/2 cup (1 stick) unsalted butter, divided

2 medium sweet onions, peeled and chopped

3/4 cup chopped button or cremini mushrooms

1/3 cup chopped roasted bell peppers

2 tablespoons chopped black olives

1/4 teaspoon salt

1 (10-ounce) package frozen puff pastry dough, thawed

1/2 cup spreadable garlic and herb cream cheese

Onions and mushrooms get along together rather well. Here, the mushrooms are more than willing to let the onions star in this appetizer. Don't rush the process of caramelizing the onions. It is worth the small time investment.

In a large skillet over medium-high heat, melt 2 tablespoons of the butter. Add the onions and cook 10 minutes or until onions are golden and caramelized, stirring occasionally. Stir in the mushrooms, peppers, olives, and salt. Cook 5 to 7 minutes longer and remove from heat. Cool at least 10 minutes.

Meanwhile, preheat the oven to 350°F.

Melt the remaining butter in a microwave-safe dish on low power. Place a sheet of the puff pastry dough on a dry work surface. Brush with half of the melted butter. With a sharp knife, cut the dough into 4-inch squares. Repeat with the remaining pastry dough and butter.

In the center of each square, place one heaping teaspoon of the onion mixture. Top with a teaspoon of cream cheese. Pull opposite corners together to form a triangle. Repeat with the remaining squares. Place on ungreased baking sheets. Bake 20 minutes or until golden brown. Serve warm.

**Note:** The filling can be made a day ahead and refrigerated. Bring to room temperature 30 minutes before using.

This dish is a tribute to our South Florida friends and the marvelous food they produce. It's a great way to kick off summer entertaining around the pool or on the deck. The crunchy, slightly sweet shrimp are enhanced with a bright, sunny dipping sauce.

~

In a Dutch oven pour the oil to a depth of 3 inches. Place over medium-high heat and bring to 350°F.

Meanwhile, make the citrus dip: Combine the marmalade, mustard, and juice in a small saucepan. Cook over medium heat, stirring constantly until the marmalade melts. Set aside.

In a medium mixing bowl, combine the biscuit mix, sugar, and beer, stirring until smooth. Place the flour and coconut in separate shallow dishes. Coat the shrimp with the flour and dip in the beer mixture. Gently roll the coated shrimp in the coconut.

Fry a few at a time until golden brown, about 2 minutes. Drain on paper towels and serve immediately with the Citrus Dip.

# Coconut Fried Shrimp and Florida Citrus Dip

**Makes 4 servings**

Vegetable oil
1 (10-ounce) jar orange marmalade
3 tablespoons spicy brown mustard
1 tablespoon lime juice
3/4 cup biscuit mix
1 tablespoon sugar
3/4 cup beer
3/4 cup all-purpose flour
2 cups shredded coconut
1 pound jumbo shrimp, peeled and deveined with tails intact

# Spotlight: Honey

## ThistleDew Farm

Ellie and Steve Conlon
Rural Route 1, Box 122
Proctor, West Virginia 26055
(800) 85-Honey or 1-800-854-6639
E-mail: info@thistledewfarm.com
Website: www.thistledewfarm.com
Consumer Experience: Purchase on-site and online

*I* love to hear stories about people who just pick up, move, and start over. That's exactly what Ellie and Steve Conlon did in 1974 when they decided to leave suburban Philadelphia and relocate to West Virginia. With their two beehives and their son, they launched a new business named ThistleDew Farm because they craved a simple life of making honey.

Flip the Conlon family album pages to this year and you'll see they've expanded that simple life considerably. Today, they have more than 700 beehives (and four sons!) that help locals and travelers alike fall in love with all the numerous ways honeybees enrich our lives.

I have always loved beautiful comb honey. There's something about seeing that comb settled amid the luscious, sweet nectar that just seems to make it taste better. The Conlons have an ample supply of the comb honey I crave, as well as shelves full of other items I really didn't know I needed.

At ThistleDew Farm, you can find honey candy that is fabulous. They also sell delicious whipped honey, for which I have found literally dozens of uses. I love their honey mustards, fruited creamed honeys, jellies, dressings, and ice cream toppings. But the real deal is the honey itself, in flavors of buckwheat, tulip poplar, orange blossom, basswood, aster, sumac, raspberry, blackberry, goldenrod, wildflower, and the tangy black locust.

There is an online store if you want to shop from your own living room. Or you can stop by Monday through Friday and have fun shopping in person. I cannot stop myself from grabbing beeswax items on the way to the checkout, like lip balms, lotions, hand creams, and of course, artisan candles. You'll be hooked too. Then, if you can pull yourself away from the hypnotic observation hive, you'll be on your way home . . . but it may be a tad later than you think!

Every time I make this spread, I find myself wondering why I don't make it more often. It looks as fresh as it tastes. It has just a bit of heat on the end, which you'll love. Select wheat crackers so the light flavor can shine.

❧

Bring a large pot of water to a boil over high heat. Place the peas in a wire basket and plunge into the boiling water. Cook 30 seconds. Drain and plunge in a sink filled with ice water. After 30 seconds, drain. Shell the peas when cool enough to handle.

In the bowl of a food processor, combine the peas, pine nuts, juice, oil, zest, cheese, cayenne, and salt. Process until smooth. Cover and refrigerate at least 15 minutes. Serve with toasted whole wheat crackers.

# Spring Green Spread

## Makes 2 cups

1 1/2 pounds fresh green peas, still in shells

1/2 cup pine nuts, toasted

1 teaspoon fresh lemon juice

1 tablespoon olive oil

1/4 teaspoon lemon zest

1/3 cup grated Parmesan cheese

1/8 teaspoon cayenne pepper (or more if desired)

1/8 teaspoon salt

This is the recipe I make as soon as the first banana peppers come in from my garden. Most often I serve it as an appetizer, but occasionally it becomes an unexpected side dish.

❧

Preheat the oven to 400°F. Line a jelly-roll pan with aluminum foil and set aside.

In a medium bowl, stir together the cream cheese, feta, parsley, oregano, and pepper. Blend until smooth and set aside.

Cut the stem end off each pepper and carefully scoop out the seeds with the blade of a knife or a small spoon. Spoon the cheese mixture into each pepper. Place on the prepared pan and drizzle with the oil. Bake 17 to 20 minutes or until the peppers are tender. Let rest 5 minutes before serving. Serve warm.

# Cheese-Filled Banana Peppers

## Makes 8 to 10 servings

4 ounces cream cheese, softened

1 cup crumbled feta cheese

1 tablespoon chopped fresh parsley

1/2 teaspoon dried oregano

1/4 teaspoon white pepper

8 large banana peppers

2 tablespoons olive oil

This salsa is perfect for tailgating and a great use for your end-of-the-year harvest of peas and peppers. This is not your normal dip or salsa, so have the recipe handy to give to friends as you serve it. I like to serve it with bagel chips or hefty low-salt pita chips.

In a large bowl, combine the peas, peppers, and onions and set aside.

In a jar with a tight-fitting lid, combine the garlic, basil, parsley, oil, vinegar, sugar, Worcestershire, salt, black pepper, and red pepper. Shake well to combine. Pour over the pea mixture, tossing to coat evenly. Cover and refrigerate overnight. Serve cold or at room temperature with crackers or chips.

# Pea–Picking Salsa

**Makes 8 servings**

1 pound fresh black-eyed peas, cooked, drained, and cooled

1 red bell pepper, roasted, peeled, seeded, and diced

1 small purple onion, peeled and diced

2 garlic cloves, minced

2 tablespoons chopped fresh basil

1 tablespoon chopped fresh parsley

3/4 cup peanut oil

1/4 cup red wine vinegar

1 1/2 teaspoons brown sugar

1 teaspoon Worcestershire sauce

1 teaspoon kosher salt

1/4 teaspoon black pepper

1/4 teaspoon crushed red pepper

# Farmers' Market

## Capitol Market

800 Smith Street
Charleston, West Virginia 25301
(304) 344-1905
E-mail: tammy@capitolmarket.net
Website: www.capitolmarket.net
Open year-round
Consumer Experience: farmers' market

*I* love farmers' markets where you can drop in any day at practically any time and stay all day. That's what I do at the Capitol Market whenever I'm close to Charleston, West Virginia. It's a favorite of those who reside nearby.

Built on an old railroad transfer dock, the market officially opened in 1997.

It plays host to a slew of specialty shops inside, and outside vendors offer everything from giant trees to the smallest berries.

The outdoor produce area seems as if it goes on for miles. You can easily and conveniently find mounds of locally grown fruits and vegetables of every persuasion. On my visit, I left with armloads of fresh corn, okra, tomatoes, eggplant, cucumbers for pickling, and heirloom beans. I was thankful I brought a cooler because once you start shopping, it is quite difficult to stop!

Wander inside and you'll find local wines, beers, cheeses, meats, chocolates, and fresh seafood. The aroma of the coffee-roasting shop alone is enough to draw you in from out of doors. The shops are eclectic and wonderfully eccentric. Since the market is open year-round, it's a fantastic stop for lunch, dinner, breakfast, brunch, an afternoon snack, or an after-work cocktail. It will put a smile on your face all throughout the day!

You will find many ways to serve this chutney. I love to place it in assorted bowls around the patio while dinner is on the grill. It is exceptional with chicken or pork and equally fantastic served as an appetizer with crackers.

⁓

Melt the butter over medium heat in a large sauté pan. Add the garlic, shallots, and jalapeños. Sauté 3 minutes. Add the peaches and raisins. Sauté 3 minutes more.

Add the sugar and vinegar, stirring well. Add the juice, salt, pepper, and hot sauce. Reduce the heat to low and simmer 7 to 10 minutes. Serve warm or at room temperature.

# Spiced Peach Chutney

**Makes 2 cups**

1 tablespoon unsalted butter

2 garlic cloves, minced

2 shallots, peeled and minced

1 jalapeño pepper, seeded and minced

3 cups chopped fresh peaches

1/2 cup golden raisins

1/4 cup sugar

1 tablespoon cider vinegar

1 tablespoon lemon juice

1 teaspoon salt

1/2 teaspoon black pepper

1/2 to 1 teaspoon hot sauce

You won't need much energy to prepare this easy-as-can-be salsa. It is beautiful served with blue corn chips and eaten on the patio while dinner is in the making inside. Leftovers can be spooned over grilled fish, chicken, or pork.

⁓

Combine the plums, peaches, honeydew, peppers, lime juice, and honey in a mixing bowl. Toss gently to evenly blend. Cover and refrigerate at least 8 hours or overnight.

Bring to room temperature around 15 minutes before serving.

**Note:** Leftovers will keep up to 5 days in the refrigerator.

# Lazy Afternoon Fruit Salsa

**Makes 1½ cups**

1 cup diced fresh plums

1/2 cup diced fresh peaches

1/2 cup diced honeydew

1 jalapeño pepper, seeded and diced

2 tablespoons lime juice

1 tablespoon honey

# Party Time Rhubarb Chutney

### Makes 2½ cups

1 pound chopped rhubarb

1 cup packed light brown sugar

1 cup white wine vinegar

½ cup golden raisins

¼ cup chopped dried apples

¼ cup chopped dried apricots

¼ cup chopped onions

3 tablespoons chopped mandarin oranges

1 garlic clove, minced

1 tablespoon chopped crystallized ginger

1 teaspoon grated orange zest

⅛ teaspoon cayenne pepper

¼ cup slivered almonds, toasted

**You could easily use this chutney as a unique cracker or bread spread, but I like to use it as an accompaniment to a cheese tray that features Gouda or Emmentaler. It is an excellent way to begin a spring party.**

In a large saucepan over medium-high heat, combine the rhubarb, sugar, vinegar, raisins, apples, apricots, onions, oranges, garlic, ginger, zest, and cayenne. Bring to a boil and reduce the heat to low. Simmer 2½ hours, stirring frequently to prevent sticking. The mixture will be thick.

Set aside to cool at least 15 minutes or allow to cool completely. Stir in the almonds just before serving.

**Note:** Store any leftovers in the refrigerator, tightly covered. Use within 1 week.

The first time I had pickled figs was on the road at a farm market in upper East Tennessee. I was instantly addicted and bought three jars. The first jar never made it back to Nashville. Incredible! Place them on an appetizer platter with low-salt crackers and slices of white Cheddar for an unforgettable treat.

❧

In a large Dutch oven over medium-high heat, place 3 cups of the sugar and the water. Stir until the sugar dissolves. Add the figs and simmer 30 minutes. Reduce the heat if necessary to keep the mixture at a slow simmer.

Add the remaining sugar and the vinegar. Tie the cinnamon, allspice, and cloves in a cheesecloth bag and add to the fig mixture. Cook gently until the figs are transparent, about 45 to 50 minutes. Cover and let stand 12 to 24 hours in the refrigerator. Remove the spice bag and discard.

Heat the fig mixture to simmering over medium heat. Pack into hot, sterilized canning jars, leaving 1/4 inch headspace. Remove any air bubbles, wipe the jar rims, and adjust the lids. Process 15 minutes in a boiling water bath. Let cool completely on a wire rack away from drafts.

# Pickled Figs

Makes 7 pints

5 cups sugar, divided
2 quarts water
4 quarts fresh figs, stemmed
3 cups distilled white vinegar
2 sticks cinnamon
1 tablespoon whole allspice
1 tablespoon whole cloves

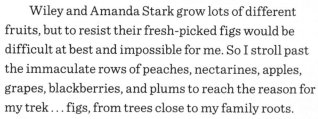

# Spotlight: Figs

## Cherry Creek Orchards

Wiley and Amanda Stark
4660 Highway 345
Pontotoc, Mississippi 38863
(662) 489-7783
E-mail: cherrycreekorchards@gmail.com
Website: www.cherrycreekorchards.com
Consumer Experience: Pick your own

Ecru, Mississippi, is where both my grandmother and mother were raised. I go back there often just to look around the tiny town and relive the many great summer memories made at my grandparents' house.

I also go there for fresh figs because the midnight-dark, remarkably rich soil of northeast Mississippi produces the best I've ever eaten. That always means a stop at Cherry Creek Orchards in Pontotoc, which is merely a stone's throw away from my childhood vacation stomping ground.

Wiley and Amanda Stark grow lots of different fruits, but to resist their fresh-picked figs would be difficult at best and impossible for me. So I stroll past the immaculate rows of peaches, nectarines, apples, grapes, blackberries, and plums to reach the reason for my trek . . . figs, from trees close to my family roots.

You can visit the orchard all summer long Monday through Saturday, but it is always best to call for availability before heading to any farm. The Starks have several fig varieties, but all have a velvet-soft flesh sprinkled with tiny edible seeds. I immediately gobble down the first ones in my possession, then squirrel away the rest in my refrigerator.

I make sure bacon is there as well to wrap around them and bake for my own version of rumaki. Then, as soon as time is on my side, they are transformed into luscious preserves that feed my fig craving long after the fresh season has passed.

This dip takes on a silky texture due to the roasting step. Add more heat if you wish by increasing the amount of crushed red pepper. It's such a nice change from ordinary cold dips and makes a great bread spread for fresh tomato sandwiches.

# Roasted Eggplant Dip

**Makes 1 1/2 cups**

1 large eggplant, peeled and cut into 1/2-inch slices
1/4 cup olive oil
1/2 teaspoon salt
1/2 teaspoon black pepper
2 garlic cloves, minced
3/4 cup sour cream
1/2 teaspoon crushed red pepper

Preheat the oven to 350°F. Place the eggplant slices on a baking sheet and drizzle both sides with the oil. Sprinkle with the salt, pepper, and garlic. Roast about 30 minutes or until very soft. Transfer to a food processor and puree. Place in a serving bowl and stir in the sour cream and red pepper. Add more salt if necessary.

Serve with whole wheat crackers or raw vegetables.

I have a feeling you will be surprised at how good this appetizer is. It looks beautiful on a serving tray and can be made ahead of time. Serve with a crisp, dry white wine, and get ready for rave reviews.

# Great Grapes

**Makes 2 dozen grapes**

1 (4-ounce) package crumbled blue cheese
4 ounces cream cheese, softened
1/4 pound seedless green grapes
1 cup finely chopped pecans, toasted

In a mixing bowl, combine the cheeses and beat until smooth. Cover and refrigerate at least 1 hour.

Wrap each grape with enough of the cheese mixture to completely cover. Place the pecans in a shallow dish. Roll the grapes in the pecans. Place in a tightly closed shallow container and refrigerate at least 1 hour before serving.

# Spring Celebration Cucumber Plates

No matter what you are celebrating—Mother's Day, graduations, wedding showers, or because winter is over—this appetizer says it's time to head outside. Cucumber slices become the serving plate for chicken and toasted pecans. It looks as Southern as it tastes.

❧

**Makes 60 appetizers**

2/3 cup diced cooked chicken
1 hard-cooked egg, finely chopped
1/2 cup mayonnaise
1/4 cup finely chopped onions
1/4 cup finely chopped green bell peppers
2 tablespoons finely chopped pecans, toasted
60 cucumber slices
60 pecan halves, toasted

In a medium bowl, combine the chicken, eggs, mayonnaise, onions, peppers, and chopped pecans. Cover and refrigerate at least 2 hours.

When ready to serve, spread 1 teaspoon of the chicken mixture on each cucumber slice. Top with a pecan half. Serve cold.

# Spotlight: Cucumbers

## Parke Family HydroFarms

Gary and Terri Parke
3715 Tanner Road
Plant City, Florida 33566
(813) 927-4049
E-mail: gary@parkehydro.com
Website: www.parkehydro.com
Consumer Experience: Pick your own, produce club

*I*magine picking a washtub full of cucumbers and never having to bend over or get dirty. That's not a dream but a reality when you arrive at Parke Family HydroFarms in Plant City, Florida. How? Because they grow hydroponically!

Hydroponic farming has been around for quite some time, but there are still many who are unfamiliar with this unique form of growing food. It was developed initially in the 1930s and replaces ordinary soil that a plant would use for growth with a liquid nutrient solution. The plants are supported with gravel and/or peat and then regularly flushed with the liquid nutrients to help them flourish.

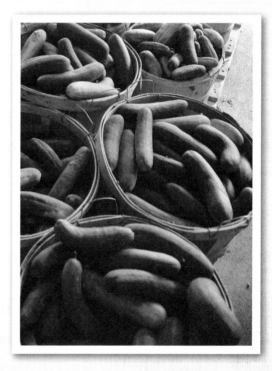

Since I like all things pickled, I was pleased as punch to run across this family farm operation for my cucumber needs. Within a cool 30 minutes, I had everything I needed for my vinegar baths to work their magic. Soon that vinegar would morph those cukes into mouthwatering pickles.

Gary's father emigrated here from Northern Ireland in the 1920s and wanted to continue his vocation of farming in his adopted country. He was obviously very good at it and passed that knowledge on to his son, who runs the business today along with his wife and four children (as they say, their only employees).

In addition to the hydroponics, the Parkes have four monstrous greenhouses that produce more than a million vegetables and flowers each year. Thanks to the indoor oasis, you can shop there year-round! It is refreshing to see this beautiful family work so well together, and I love the results of their labor.

# Kernels of Wisdom Salsa

**Winter salsa doesn't have to be tasteless and from a jar. This one uses items you probably already have in the freezer or pantry, and it feeds a crowd.**

### Makes 8 cups

1 1/3 cups whole kernel corn

3 1/2 cups cooked crowder or black-eyed peas

2 (10-ounce) cans diced tomatoes and green chiles

1 1/2 cups diced fresh tomatoes

6 green onions, chopped

1 (16-ounce) bottle zesty Italian dressing

2 garlic cloves, minced

2 tablespoons chopped fresh parsley

Blue corn chips

In a large bowl, combine the corn, peas, tomatoes and green chiles, tomatoes, onions, dressing, garlic, and parsley. Cover and refrigerate 8 hours. Drain before serving with blue corn chips.

# Time-Honored Cheese Crackers

**This appetizer has been welcoming guests into Southern homes for centuries. I cannot make it through the holidays without making several batches. Plus, it makes a well-received hostess gift!**

### Makes 7 1/2 dozen

1 pound sharp Cheddar cheese, shredded and at room temperature

1 1/2 cups all-purpose flour

4 tablespoons unsalted butter, softened

1 teaspoon salt

1/4 teaspoon cayenne pepper

Preheat the oven to 375°F.

Place the cheese, flour, butter, salt, and cayenne in the bowl of a food processor. Process 30 seconds or until the mixture forms a ball. Transfer the dough to a cookie press fitted with a star disc.

Following the manufacturer's directions, press the straws onto ungreased baking sheets. Bake 8 to 10 minutes or until very lightly browned. Cool on wire racks. Store in an airtight container.

## Spotlight: Goat Cheese

### Bonnie Blue Farm

Gayle and Jim Tanner
257 Dry Creek Road
Waynesboro, Tennessee 38485
(931) 722-GOAT (4628)
E-mail: tanngoat@wildblue.net
Website: http://www.bonniebluefarm.com
Consumer Experience: Tours, lodging, purchase on farm,
purchase in retail outlets, purchase at local farmers' markets

Gayle and Jim Tanner moved to the South from Northern California more than ten years ago. They bought a rolling 300-acre farm in Waynesboro, Tennessee, where their herd of goats wanders freely, nibbling on grass and dozing in the shade.

The couple makes incredibly creamy goat cheese on-site, and their Bonnie Blue Farm was the first licensed goat dairy in the state of Tennessee. These award-winning fresh, handmade cheeses have a flavor that is unique and marvelous.

The cheese stands apart from the mass-produced products you typically find on grocery store shelves. Even those who think they don't like goat cheese have had their minds quickly change with just a taste of this farm-fresh product.

Visit Bonnie Blue Farm year-round and you'll see firsthand how the cheese is made in their "cheese studio." In addition, they have log cabins for those who really want to escape the hustle and bustle of city life and want to see how a working cheese farm operates on a daily basis. You will love the educational experience! So whether it's for a day or for a weekend, it's a delicious way to invest your time in agriculture.

# Golden Brown Goat Cheese Medallions

**Makes 6 servings**

1 tablespoon olive oil
1 egg
1/8 teaspoon salt
1/8 teaspoon black pepper
1 cup dry plain breadcrumbs
1 (10.5-ounce) log plain goat cheese

I love to serve these crispies as an appetizer any time of the year. At dinner, they are perfect with a simple tossed salad. It's like a cheese crouton.

Position the oven rack to the highest place in the oven. Preheat the oven to 400°F. Brush a baking sheet with the oil and set aside.

In a small, shallow bowl, whisk together the egg, salt, and pepper. Place the breadcrumbs in another shallow bowl.

Slice the goat cheese into 12 equal rounds. Dip each round into the egg mixture, then the breadcrumbs. If necessary, pat gently to evenly coat each round. Place on the prepared baking sheet and bake 5 minutes or until crisp and golden brown. Serve immediately.

# Spring Street Bean Spread

### Makes 4 cups

2 cups fresh baby lima beans

1 large yellow onion, peeled and chopped

5 garlic cloves, peeled

1 teaspoon seasoned salt

2 cups water

1/4 cup chopped cilantro

1/4 cup chopped fresh parsley

1/4 teaspoon cayenne pepper

3 tablespoons lemon juice

1/4 cup olive oil

2 tablespoons chopped fresh dill

1/4 teaspoon black pepper

Fresh cilantro for garnish

George and I laugh because we believe every Southern town has a Spring Street. And every Southern home should have an herb garden to accent this bean spread that can double as a dip. It's particularly good tightly rolled in spinach or tomato tortillas and sliced for a unique finger food.

❧

In a large saucepan over medium-high heat, combine the beans, onions, garlic, salt, and 2 cups of water. Bring to a simmer, cover, and cook 8 minutes or until the beans are tender.

Remove from the heat and add the cilantro and parsley, stirring to blend. Let stand 5 minutes. Drain and transfer to the bowl of a food processor.

Add the cayenne, juice, oil, dill, and pepper. Process until smooth. Transfer to a serving bowl and cool to room temperature. Refrigerate until ready to use or garnish with cilantro and serve at room temperature with crackers.

Want an out-of-the-ordinary appetizer for your next dinner party? Serve this as a first course with cheese and wine! Then don't be surprised when guests want the recipe. I made this thinking I would give it a try just once . . . That was years ago, and I make it every year in the fall to kick off the change in seasons.

༄

In a large saucepan over medium-high heat, combine the apples, sugar, vinegar, apricots, peaches, pears, raisins, garlic, ginger, salt, and cayenne. Bring to a boil and reduce heat to medium.

Simmer 35 to 40 minutes, stirring often. Cool to room temperature. Spoon into canning jars and refrigerate 2 weeks before using. Serve cold or at room temperature.

**Note:** This chutney will keep 2 months in the refrigerator.

# Good to the Core Apple Chutney

**Makes 3 1/4 cups**

5 Granny Smith or Newtown Pippin apples, cored, peeled, and chopped

2 1/2 cups sugar

1 1/4 cups red wine vinegar

1/2 cup dried apricots, chopped

1/2 cup dried peaches, chopped

1/2 cup dried pears, chopped

1/3 cup golden raisins

6 garlic cloves, minced

1 tablespoon grated fresh ginger

2 teaspoons salt

3/4 teaspoon cayenne pepper

**The sweet-and-salty mixture of this snack is perfect for times when it's too long until the next meal. Substitute walnut halves for the pecans if you desire. This recipe can be easily doubled.**

≈

Preheat the oven to 350°F. Spread the pecans in a single layer on a jelly-roll pan. Drizzle with the butter. Sprinkle the bacon pieces evenly over the pecans. Bake 25 minutes or until the bacon is done, stirring occasionally.

Meanwhile, in a small bowl, combine the sugar and salt. As soon as the pecans come out of the oven, sprinkle evenly with the sugar mixture. Cool on a wire rack. Serve at room temperature.

**Note:** Store leftovers in the refrigerator and bring to room temperature before serving.

# Roasted Bacon Pecans

**Makes 2 cups**

2 cups pecan halves

2 tablespoons unsalted butter, melted

6 bacon slices, chopped

2 tablespoons sugar

$1/2$ teaspoon salt

# "Where's the Party?" Broccoli Dip

This dip looks like Christmas, with colorful speckles of green and red mixed throughout the warm, creamy dip. It can certainly get the holiday party season started. Serve with sturdy crackers.

☙

Preheat the oven to 350°F. In a medium bowl, combine the broccoli, pimientos, Parmesan, mayonnaise, 1/2 cup of the mozzarella, hot sauce, salt, pepper, and paprika. Spread in a lightly greased 1-quart baking dish.

Bake 20 minutes and sprinkle with the remaining mozzarella. Bake 5 minutes longer or until the cheese is melted. Serve warm with crackers.

**Makes 3 cups**

1 1/2 cups chopped broccoli

1 (2-ounce) jar chopped pimientos, drained

1/2 cup shredded Parmesan cheese

1 cup mayonnaise

1 cup shredded mozzarella, divided

1 teaspoon hot sauce

1/4 teaspoon garlic salt

1/4 teaspoon black pepper

1/4 teaspoon paprika

Don't let the fresh peach season bypass you before making this incredible summer fruit salsa. It is terrific on grilled fish or chicken as well as a premeal treat with blue corn chips. It benefits from time in the refrigerator before serving.

Place the peaches, onions, and peppers in a medium serving bowl and gently mix. In a small jar with a tight-fitting lid, combine the juice, oil, salt, and pepper, shaking well to emulsify. Pour over the peach mixture, tossing gently to evenly coat.

Cover and refrigerate at least 2 hours before serving. Bring to room temperature and toss well before using.

# Fresh Peach Salsa

## Makes 4 cups

6 fresh peaches, pitted and diced

1/2 cup diced purple onions

1/3 cup diced red bell peppers

2 tablespoons lime juice

2 tablespoons olive oil

1/4 teaspoon salt

1/8 teaspoon black pepper

# Soups

Cold Summer Peach Soup

Gulf Coast Corn and Shrimp Soup

Spring Festival Lamb Soup

Garden Vegetable Soup

Swizzle Stick Soup

Crab and White Corn Soup

Grilled Gazpacho

Fall Squash and Sausage Soup

Turnip Harvest Soup

Sweet Potato and Shrimp Chowder

First Cold Night Corn and Potato Chowder

Roasted Sweet Potato Soup

Smoked Tomato Soup

# Cold Summer Peach Soup

**Makes 6⅓ cups**

2½ pounds fresh peaches, peeled and pitted

3 cups cream

2 tablespoons pear or raspberry vinegar

⅓ cup plus 1 tablespoon honey

**Hot weather means cold menus in the South. This soup is simply terrific with chicken salad for lunch or served as a light dessert.**

In the bowl of a food processor or blender, process the peaches until smooth. Transfer to a large saucepan and stir in the cream, vinegar, and honey. Place over medium heat and simmer 5 minutes, stirring frequently.

Remove from the heat and cool to room temperature. Cover and refrigerate 8 hours or overnight, stirring occasionally. Bring to room temperature 15 minutes before serving.

# Gulf Coast Corn and Shrimp Soup

**Makes 6 to 8 servings**

1 tablespoon olive oil

¼ cup chopped green onions

1 garlic clove, minced

¼ teaspoon black pepper

2 (10.75-ounce) cans cream of potato soup

2 cups milk or half-and-half

3 ounces cream cheese, softened

1 cup whole kernel sweet corn

1 pound medium shrimp, peeled and deveined

**This soup comes together in a flash and is one of the fastest ways I have to put dinner on the table. It really takes the chill off if you serve it with hot sauce.**

Place the oil in a large Dutch oven over medium-high heat. Add the onions, garlic, and pepper. Sauté 3 to 4 minutes or until tender.

Stir in the soup, milk, cheese, and corn. Reduce the heat to medium and bring to a boil, stirring occasionally. Add the shrimp, cover, and reduce the heat to low. Cook 4 to 5 minutes longer or until the shrimp are no longer pink. Serve immediately.

## Lane Southern Orchards

Duke Lane III
50 Lane Road (Highway 96 East)
Fort Valley, Georgia 31030
(800) 27-Peach or 1-800-277-3224
Website: www.lanesouthernorchards.com
Consumer Experience: Tour, farm market, lunch
restaurant, purchase online

Right smack-dab in the middle of the state of Georgia is a 5,000-acre farm where you can find juice-filled fruit that will leave you wonderfully sticky from your chin to your elbows. It's Lane Southern Orchards, aka Georgia Peach Heaven.

It all began in 1908, in Fort Valley, Georgia, where John David Duke not only grew beautiful fresh peaches, but also made the wooden baskets he shipped them in. Over the years, the orchard size grew and grew and grew.

The orchards' produce packinghouse, which was completed in 1990, is one of the finest I've ever visited. It has the capacity to pack and ship a million 25-pound cartons of fresh Georgia peaches every year during the growing season. It is quite a remarkably modern operation to watch and is brilliantly efficient at every turn. To tour it is totally mesmerizing.

The fifth-generation family members who are still involved in the day-to-day farm operation now welcome more than 300,000 visitors every year, and *you* need to be one of them. It's always convenient to go by to shop and visit because they are open year-round. In addition to the postcard-perfect orchards, there are a bakery, catering facility, lunch restaurant, and a farm market.

You can even shop online if you have a craving and don't happen to be anywhere near Fort Valley, Georgia. The homemade peach cobbler is only matched by the hand-churned peach ice cream. Both taste like something from your grandmother's kitchen.

# Spring Festival Lamb Soup

**Makes 6 to 8 servings**

3 pounds boneless lamb shoulder, cubed

3 tablespoons all-purpose flour

1 teaspoon fine sea salt

1 teaspoon black pepper

1 tablespoon olive oil

5 garlic cloves, minced

1 1/2 cups dry white wine

2 cups beef stock

1/2 cup orange juice

2 tablespoons chopped fresh thyme

1 1/2 tablespoons chopped fresh rosemary

1 pound baby carrots

1 pound fresh or 1 (16-ounce) bag frozen whole pearl onions, unthawed

1/2 pound fresh green peas

1 tablespoon chopped fresh parsley

**Here come those early vegetables again, but this time you use green peas, pearl onions, and baby carrots to give lamb a humble base for this soup. It is a delicious vehicle for introducing those who are not quite convinced to try lamb. They will be glad they did!**

Place the lamb in a large zip-top plastic bag. Add the flour, salt, and pepper. Shake to evenly coat.

Heat the oil in a large Dutch oven over medium-high heat. Add the lamb and cook 5 to 7 minutes, stirring constantly. Add the garlic and cook 2 minutes longer.

Stir in the wine and cook 5 minutes. Add the stock, juice, thyme, and rosemary and bring to a boil. Reduce the heat to low, cover, and simmer 2 hours, stirring occasionally.

Add the carrots and onions. Cook 10 minutes, uncovered. Stir in the peas and cook 15 minutes longer. Ladle into warm soup bowls and garnish with the parsley.

This is soup at the peak of freshness. It's about as old-fashioned as soup can get and perfectly loaded with plenty of summer vegetables. Left-overs freeze beautifully, so on a rainy summer weekend, plan for the winter months ahead and you'll be grateful you made the time to do so in January!

❧

Place the olive oil in a large Dutch oven over medium heat. Add the onions, celery, and garlic. Cook 4 minutes. Add the potatoes, carrots, peppers, turnips, corn, beans, peas, stock, wine, oregano, parsley, salt, and pepper. Bring to a boil and reduce heat to low, stirring occasionally. Simmer 1 hour or until the vegetables are tender. Serve hot.

# Garden Vegetable Soup

Makes 8 to 10 servings

1 tablespoon vegetable or olive oil

1 yellow onion, peeled and diced

2 celery stalks, diced

1 garlic clove, minced

4 Yukon Gold potatoes, peeled and diced

3 carrots, peeled and diced

1 green bell pepper, seeded and diced

1 turnip, peeled and diced

1 cup whole kernel sweet corn

1 cup snapped green beans

1 cup fresh green peas

5 cups vegetable stock

$1/2$ cup dry white wine

1 teaspoon dry crushed oregano

$1/4$ cup chopped fresh parsley

$1/2$ teaspoon salt

$1/2$ teaspoon black pepper

Those fun glass swizzle sticks that you rarely use in drinks have a new use with this soup. They are the perfect size and shape for beautifully garnishing this yummy concoction. And the soup looks much prettier than if you used a knife blade to swirl in the yogurt. I like this soup served cold, but you can also serve it at room temperature.

# Swizzle Stick Soup

**Makes 8 to 10 servings**

3 pounds fresh peaches or apricots, pitted, peeled, and halved

3 cups peach or apricot nectar

1 cup dry white wine

1 teaspoon ground ginger

Pinch of saffron threads

1/2 cup honey

1/2 cup firmly packed light brown sugar

1/4 teaspoon kosher salt

1 cup half-and-half

1/2 cup plain yogurt

Mint sprigs for garnish

In a Dutch oven over medium-high heat, combine the peaches, nectar, wine, ginger, and saffron. Bring to a boil. Reduce the heat to low and simmer 30 minutes.

Remove from the heat and add the honey, brown sugar, salt, and half-and-half. Using an immersion blender, puree the soup until smooth. (Or cool and puree in a regular blender.)

Ladle into soup bowls. Place a dollop of yogurt in the center of each bowl. With a swizzle stick, swirl the yogurt, and garnish with fresh mint. Serve warm, at room temperature, or chilled.

Use corn you've frozen from the summer harvest or bought for this quick cold-weather dinner dish. If the corn is frozen loosely packed, there is no need to thaw. All it needs is a loaf of crusty bread to sop up the juices.

# Crab and White Corn Soup

**Makes 4 servings**

2 cups white corn kernels, divided
1 cup milk
1 (8-ounce) bottle clam juice
3 green onions, chopped
1 teaspoon fresh ginger, peeled and minced
4 teaspoons lemon juice, divided
1/4 teaspoon salt
1/4 teaspoon white pepper
2 tablespoons unsalted butter
6 ounces cooked crabmeat, flaked
1 tablespoon chopped fresh parsley

Reserve 1/4 cup of the corn. Bring the remaining corn and milk to a boil in a medium saucepan over medium-high heat. Cover, remove from the heat, and let stand 10 minutes.

With an immersion blender (or cool first and process in a regular blender), puree the corn mixture. Stir in the clam juice, onions, and ginger. Puree again until nearly smooth. Bring to a simmer over medium heat and add 1 1/2 teaspoons of the lemon juice as well as the salt and pepper.

In a small skillet over medium heat, melt the butter. As soon as it begins to foam, add the reserved corn and sauté 1 minute. Stir in the crabmeat and the remaining lemon juice.

To serve, ladle the soup into warm bowls. Mound the crab mixture on the top and sprinkle with the fresh parsley. Serve immediately.

## Spotlight: Tomatoes

### Charlie's U-Pik

Charlie Eubanks
257 Charlie's Lane
Lucedale, Mississippi 39452
(601) 530-0548
E-mail: info@charliesupik.com
Website: www.charliesupik.com
Consumer Experience: Pick your own, farm market

Most people plant things because they love the process of fertilizing, watering, weeding, and eventually harvesting. Others plant because they have a vision for growing more than produce. Charlie Eubanks is the latter, and his vision for growing a few tomatoes for his family and friends has expanded to include a whole community.

Back in the 1990s Charlie found that his tomato-growing hobby had blossomed to cover 10 acres. He opened it up to the public, and Charlie's U-Pik was born. Today, it occupies 100 acres overflowing with tomatoes, as well as peppers, beans, squash, cucumbers, eggplant, onions, peas, okra, and zucchini. Go there in June and you'll find yourself returning all summer long for Charlie's fresh feast of vegetables.

But tomatoes remain in the spotlight for me, and deservedly so. I am particularly drawn to the heirloom varieties grown there. A few decades ago, some devoted horticulturists began collecting seeds of older, lesser-known varieties, and these seeds have slowly become a source of paradise for produce connoisseurs.

Heirloom tomatoes are, simply put, fantastic. They don't look as "perfect" as mass-produced types, but one slice or bite makes up for it. You'll find a rainbow of colors and sizes that range from tiny to ones where one sliver from the middle will cover an entire sandwich.

When you hit the Mississippi line, head south to Greene County and look for the signs pointing you to Charlie's. It will do you good to step from the car, stretch, and start picking. Later, as you drive away, you'll be glad you stopped, and you'll have a new appreciation for those who have a vision.

The grill adds another layer of flavor to this dish that can't happen if it's done completely in one pot. I love the colorful spoonfuls and the versatility of this gazpacho. It can be used as a soup, a salsa, or a pasta topping.

~

Preheat the grill to medium-high heat (375°F). Arrange the tomatoes, onions, zucchini, bell peppers, garlic bulb, and jalapeño in a greased grilling basket. Grill with the lid closed for 15 to 20 minutes or until lightly charred, turning every 5 minutes.

Remove from the grill and place the bell peppers in a large zip-top plastic bag. Seal and let stand 10 minutes. Remove and discard the skins. Squeeze the garlic from the bulb and discard the outer peel. Cut the jalapeño in half, discarding the stem and seeds.

Process all the vegetables in batches in a food processor until coarsely chopped. Transfer to a large serving bowl and add the tomato juice, tomatoes and green chiles, cilantro, lime juice, sugar, salt, chervil, cumin, and pepper. Cover and refrigerate overnight. Serve cold or at room temperature.

**Note:** Gazpacho can be frozen up to 6 months. Thaw in the refrigerator overnight.

# Grilled Gazpacho

**Makes 4 quarts**

12 Roma tomatoes

4 medium sweet onions, peeled and quartered

2 zucchini, cut in half and seeded

1 red bell pepper, cut in half and seeded

1 garlic bulb, with 1/4 inch of the pointed top removed

1 jalapeño

1 (32-ounce) can tomato juice

2 (10-ounce) cans diced tomatoes and green chiles

1/3 cup chopped cilantro

3 tablespoons lime juice

1 teaspoon sugar

1 teaspoon seasoned salt

1 teaspoon dried chervil

1 teaspoon cumin

1/2 teaspoon black pepper

# Fall Squash and Sausage Soup

**Makes 8 servings**

1 large butternut, acorn, Hubbard or other fall squash, peeled, seeded, and cut into large dice

2 tablespoons olive oil

1 tablespoon unsalted butter

2 sweet onions, peeled and cut into large dice

6 garlic cloves

1 cup dry red wine

8 cups chicken stock

1 pound hot or sage pork sausage, cooked and crumbled

1 tablespoon Worcestershire sauce

1 tablespoon hot sauce

2 teaspoons chopped fresh thyme

2 teaspoons chopped fresh oregano

1/2 teaspoon salt

1/2 teaspoon black pepper

**Let the temperatures dip to where I need a sleeve at night and I'm ready to make this satisfying soup. I especially like that it fulfills and fills up empty tummies. It freezes beautifully if you have any leftovers.**

Preheat the oven to 350°F. Place the squash on a roasting pan and drizzle with the oil. Bake 25 to 30 minutes or until tender and slightly caramelized.

Meanwhile, heat the butter in a large stockpot over medium-high heat. As soon as it foams, add the onions and sauté until tender and browned, about 12 minutes. Add the garlic and wine. Cook until the wine is reduced by half, about 15 minutes.

Add the roasted squash and stock and bring to a boil. Reduce the heat to low and simmer 15 minutes longer. Strain the squash mixture through a fine sieve. Puree the solids and return the puree to the stockpot.

Add the sausage, Worcestershire, hot sauce, thyme, oregano, salt, and pepper. Heat thoroughly and serve warm.

With one bite, everyone will think you have added a secret ingredient to potato soup. Oh, there is a secret ingredient, all right . . . no potatoes, but turnips! This is a recipe you'll reach for over and over again. It is an inexpensive yet glorious dinner.

In a large Dutch oven over medium-high heat, combine the turnips, stock, garlic, and shallots. Bring to a boil, cover, and reduce the heat to medium-low. Simmer 25 minutes or until the turnips are tender.

With an immersion blender (or cool and puree in a regular blender), puree the turnip mixture until smooth. Stir in the butter, salt, pepper, cayenne, and cream. Cook 5 minutes longer or until thoroughly heated. Serve in warm soup bowls with a garnish of chives and bacon.

# Turnip Harvest Soup

Makes 1½ quarts

6 turnips, peeled and cubed

4 cups chicken stock

1 garlic clove, peeled

1 shallot, peeled and chopped

2 tablespoons unsalted butter, softened

1/2 teaspoon salt

1/4 teaspoon black pepper

1/4 teaspoon cayenne pepper

1/4 cup cream

Chopped fresh chives

Chopped cooked bacon

# Sweet Potato and Shrimp Chowder

**This chowder isn't your typical heavy, thick fare. Instead, it has a delicate broth that is accented with seared sweet potatoes. It is excellent in the fall and even better in the early spring with a fresh green side salad.**

#### Makes 6 servings

8 bacon slices, diced
1 white onion, peeled and diced
3 sweet potatoes, peeled and diced
1 cup dry red wine
3 cups chicken stock
1 1/2 pounds small shrimp, cooked
8 green onions, thinly sliced
2 teaspoons chopped fresh parsley
2 tablespoons sour cream
1/2 teaspoon salt
1/4 teaspoon black pepper

Place a Dutch oven over medium heat. When hot, add the bacon and fry until crispy, around 3 minutes. With a slotted spoon, transfer to paper towels. Set aside.

Add the onions to the pan drippings and cook without stirring about 5 minutes or until they begin to brown. Add the sweet potatoes and cook without stirring about 5 minutes or until they begin to brown.

Add the wine and reduce 5 minutes. Add the stock and cook 10 minutes or until the sweet potatoes are tender. Meanwhile, in a separate bowl, combine the shrimp, green onions, and parsley and set aside. Gently fold the sour cream, salt, and pepper into the sweet potato mixture.

Ladle the chowder into warm shallow bowls. Evenly distribute the shrimp mixture and the cooked bacon over the top. Serve warm.

I make this recipe every year as soon as it gets the least bit cold outside. It ushers in the new season beautifully with comfort food in the form of a soup. Serve it with slow-simmered, grass-fed beef.

❧

In a large saucepan over medium heat, combine the oil and butter. When hot, add the onions, bell peppers, celery, corn, chiles, and potatoes. Cook 9 minutes.

In a small bowl, combine the flour, chili powder, salt, cayenne, pepper, and cumin. Stir into the corn mixture. Cook 1 minute, stirring constantly. Add the stock, mix well, and bring to a boil. Reduce the heat to low and simmer uncovered for 5 minutes, stirring occasionally.

Add the cream and cook 8 minutes longer, stirring frequently until the soup thickens. Ladle into warm soup bowls and serve immediately.

# First Cold Night Corn and Potato Chowder

**Makes 8 servings**

2 tablespoons olive oil

1 tablespoon unsalted butter

3/4 cup chopped purple onions

1/2 cup chopped red bell peppers

1/2 cup chopped celery

2 cups whole kernel sweet corn

1 (4.5-ounce) can chopped green chiles

3 medium russet potatoes, peeled and shredded

2 tablespoons all-purpose flour

1 teaspoon chili powder

1/2 teaspoon garlic salt

1/4 teaspoon cayenne pepper

1/4 teaspoon black pepper

1/4 teaspoon ground cumin

2 1/2 cups chicken stock

3/4 cup cream or half-and-half, room temperature

# Roasted Sweet Potato Soup

## Makes 8 servings

5 sweet potatoes, peeled and diced
3 tablespoons olive oil
6 peppered bacon slices, diced
4 white onions, peeled and julienned
3 garlic cloves, minced
1 cup dry white wine
8 cups chicken stock
1 tablespoon hot sauce
1 tablespoon Worcestershire sauce
$1/2$ teaspoon salt
$1/4$ teaspoon black pepper
3 tablespoons sour cream

**This rustic soup pairs the sweetest potatoes with caramelized onions. It is perfect for a light dinner outside before a fire, served in soup mugs.**

Preheat the oven to 375°F. Place the sweet potatoes on a lightly greased jelly-roll pan and toss gently with the oil. Roast 45 minutes.

Halfway through the roasting time, place a large Dutch oven over medium heat and fry the bacon until crisp, around 4 minutes. Drain the bacon on paper towels. Set aside.

Add the onions to the pan drippings and cook 15 minutes or until they begin to turn brown. Add the garlic and wine. Increase the heat to medium-high and simmer 10 minutes.

Add the sweet potatoes and stock. Bring to a boil, reduce the heat to low, and simmer 25 minutes. Using an immersion blender (or cool and use a regular blender), puree the soup until smooth.

Stir in the hot sauce, Worcestershire, salt, and pepper. Ladle into warm soup bowls and garnish with the sour cream and reserved bacon. Serve warm.

### Stanley Farms

R. T. Stanley
3309 East First Street
Vidalia, Georgia 30474
(912) 526-3575 or 1-800-673-6338
E-mail: contact@stanleyonions.com
Website: www.vidaliavalley.com
Consumer Experience: Farm market, purchase online,
purchase at retail outlets

*I*f you live in Georgia, chances are you intimately know about the exceptional onions produced by Stanley Farms in Vidalia. R. T. Stanley's family farm is synonymous with the sweet onions his part of Georgia has become famous for around the world.

R. T. began farming as a sharecropper in 1964 and has grown from those humble beginnings to more than 1,000 acres of sweet onions alone. That doesn't include the other crops and vegetables grown there, as well as the 100 acres of certified organic onions he produces. R. T. grew his first sweet onions in 1975 and is now regarded as a premier grower and expert in the field. He knows the sandy loam soils of Toombs County in southeast Georgia, and the three inches of rain they receive during the growing season are perfect for onion growing.

Today R. T.'s three sons, Brian, Tracy, and Vince, are helping propel the operation to recognition as the source of the world's sweetest onions. Their vertical marketing company processes countless Vidalia onion products, like yummy relishes, salad dressings, barbecue sauces, steak sauces, hot sauces, and salsas. I am hooked on the Vidalia Onion Blossom Sauce! As a cook, I appreciate the flash-frozen diced or sliced frozen Vidalias, as well as the battered frozen Vidalia onion rings. I have sugar-sweet onions to use in recipes through the entire year. And if I start to run low on anything, I can thank their online store for keeping me in onions and that fantastic sauce.

This soup is richly intense with more depth of flavor than you've ever had in a tomato soup. Just add a grilled cheese sandwich and dinner is ready!

꿍

Soak the hickory chips in water at least 1 hour. Drain and place in the bottom of a large, disposable aluminum pan. Place a baking rack that has been coated with cooking spray on top of the chips.

Preheat the grill to medium. Arrange the tomatoes on the prepared rack. Sprinkle the cut tops with 4 tablespoons of the oil. Cover with heavy-duty aluminum foil and grill 20 minutes. Cool 15 minutes. Remove and discard the tomato skins.

Place 1/4 cup of the oil, as well as the leeks and onions in a soup pot. Cook over medium-high heat 10 minutes. Crush or roughly chop the tomatoes. Add the tomatoes, wine, bacon, garlic, salt, vinegar, pepper, and cayenne to the pot. Cook over medium heat 15 minutes.

Add the parsley and stir in the remaining oil. Use an immersion blender to puree the soup (or cool slightly and puree in a regular blender in small batches). Divide evenly among warm soup bowls and float croutons on top. Serve immediately.

**Note:** Leeks can be difficult to clean because sand and soil gets stuck in between the layers of growth. To make sure my guests don't end up with a mouthful of sand, I always slice the leeks and place them in a bowl of cold water. All the dirt will fall to the bottom of the bowl and the leeks can be scooped out and dried off before cooking.

# Smoked Tomato Soup

### Makes 6 to 8 servings

2 cups hickory wood smoking chips

12 ripe tomatoes, with 1/8-inch of tops removed

1/2 cup plus 4 tablespoons olive oil, divided

2 cups diced leeks (white and light green parts)

1 cup chopped yellow onions

1 cup dry red wine

2 tablespoons diced smoked bacon

5 garlic cloves, minced

2 tablespoons fine sea salt

1 tablespoon red wine vinegar

1/4 teaspoon black pepper

1/4 teaspoon cayenne pepper

1/4 cup chopped fresh parsley

Cornbread Croutons (page 63)

# Salads

Mixed Herb Croutons

Roasted Asparagus Seafood Salad with
  Creamy Herb Drizzle

BLT Layered Salad

Fresh Peach Vinaigrette

Eggplant and Sweet Onion Salad

Hot Bacon Dressing over Wilted Greens

Fresh Beet Vinaigrette over Iceberg Wedges

Tomato Bread Salad

Hot Cilantro Dressing over Mesclun Greens

Cornbread Croutons

Blueberry Horseradish Vinaigrette

Warm Fig Dressing on Parmesan Greens

Grilled Corn Salad

Dilled Crawfish Salad

Ruby Raspberry Vinegar

Cherry Rice Salad

Candied Carrot Dressing with Bibb Lettuce

Honeyed Buttermilk Dressing over Mixed Greens

Fresh Spinach and Bacon Salad

# Mixed Herb Croutons

### Makes 4 cups

8 slices bread

1 tablespoon olive oil

1/4 teaspoon salt

1/4 teaspoon black pepper

4 garlic cloves, minced

3 tablespoons minced fresh parsley

2 tablespoons minced fresh basil

1 tablespoon minced fresh oregano

2 teaspoons minced fresh thyme

2 teaspoons water

Store-bought croutons will instantly become an item you *used* to buy when you taste these easy homemade substitutes. It's a great way to use leftover bread of any type, so never throw away pieces. Just freeze them until you have enough to make a whole batch. I've even used raisin bread to make sweet croutons.

❧

Preheat the oven to 375°F. Lightly grease a baking sheet and set aside.

Lightly brush each side of the bread with the oil. Cut into cubes and spread in a single layer on the prepared sheet.

In a small bowl, combine the salt, pepper, and garlic. Sprinkle evenly over the cubes. Bake 12 to 14 minutes or until toasted.

Meanwhile, in the same small bowl, combine the parsley, basil, oregano, thyme, and water. Mix well. Sprinkle evenly over the toasted croutons. Bake 3 to 4 minutes longer. Cool completely on a wire rack.

**Note:** Store in an airtight container at room temperature.

# Lavender Fields Herb Farm

Stan and Nicole Schermerhorn
11300 Winfrey Road
Glen Allen, Virginia 23059
(804) 262-7167
Website: www.lavenderfieldsfarm.com
Consumer Experience: Tours, classes, tearoom,
purchase on-site

Tucked into 21 beautiful acres bordered by the Chickahominy River sits Lavender Fields Herb Farm. Central Virginia is the perfect setting for this exquisite farm, and you'll find yourself instantly relaxed as soon as you arrive.

Stan and Nicole Shermerhorn have created aromatherapy bliss with their fresh herb farm. It has the largest selection of organic herbs in the area, and as you stroll through their gardens, you'll suddenly have a need for a lot more herbs than you originally dreamed you wanted or needed. I know because it happens to me every time I go there!

What I especially love is their dedication to educating their customers. Staff are ready to help with any question you could possibly have, and they are remarkably helpful, even when the place is extra crowded. The gift shop is lovely, with all sorts of soaps, teas, potpourri, and sachets.

The farm is closed during the months of January and February but open the remainder of the year. Call or go online for their operating hours as well as to check the class schedule and for upcoming special events.

Aside from the herbs, my favorite reason to visit the Shermerhorns' farm is the local honey. Bob Stapleton is the local beekeeper who religiously harvests beehives strategically located throughout the property. In fact, he is responsible for around 350 pounds annually, and it is magnificent. I love to purchase raw honey with the comb in the jar. It looks both rustic and natural.

So get ready to garden with fresh herbs! Head to Lavender Fields Herb Farm with your list of necessary herbs, grab some local honey, shop, and have a leisurely lunch in their tearoom. You'll be sensationally refreshed and ready to hit the herb garden ground running when you leave there.

# Roasted Asparagus Seafood Salad with Creamy Herb Drizzle

**Makes 6 servings**

1 cup dry white wine

1 garlic clove, minced

Pinch of saffron

1 pound fish fillets, such as halibut or tilapia

1 pound peeled shrimp

1/4 pound fresh crabmeat

1/4 cup white wine vinegar

1 small shallot, peeled and diced

1 tablespoon Dijon mustard

2 teaspoons chopped fresh thyme

2 teaspoons chopped fresh parsley

1/2 cup plus 2 tablespoons olive oil, divided

1/4 teaspoon garlic salt

1/4 teaspoon black pepper

1 1/2 pounds trimmed fresh asparagus

6 large lettuce leaves

Every year, on May 8, I honor my grandmother's birthday with a dinner featuring this dish. I really don't know why or how I started the tradition, but it's elegant and beautiful, just like she was while here on earth. Use it as a way to show your own family how special they are to you on any day.

Heat a large sauté pan over medium heat. Add the wine, garlic, and saffron. When hot, add the fillets. Simmer 4 to 5 minutes or until the fish is done. Transfer to a mixing bowl and break apart the fish with the spatula. Add the shrimp to the skillet, cooking 3 to 4 minutes or just until cooked through. Transfer the shrimp to the mixing bowl and fold in the crab. Refrigerate until ready to use.

In a small bowl, whisk together the vinegar, shallots, mustard, thyme, and parsley. Add 1/2 cup of the oil and continue to whisk until smooth. Season with the garlic salt and pepper. Refrigerate, covered, until ready to serve.

Preheat the oven to 350°F. Place the asparagus on a jelly-roll pan and drizzle with the remaining oil. Cook until the asparagus is al dente, about 15 minutes depending on the thickness of the spears. Distribute the lettuce leaves and asparagus on serving plates; then top with seafood salad. Drizzle with the dressing and serve immediately.

You love it as a sandwich and you'll equally love it in the form of this beautiful layered salad. It transports well, so take it to family get-togethers all season long.

୧୧

In a medium bowl, combine the mayonnaise, sour cream, juice, basil, salt, and pepper. Whisk until smooth and set aside.

Layer the lettuce, bacon, and tomatoes in a 13 x 9-inch baking dish. Evenly spread the mayonnaise mixture over the top. Cover and refrigerate at least 2 hours before serving. Sprinkle with croutons just before serving.

# BLT Layered Salad

**Makes 8 servings**

1 cup mayonnaise

1 (8-ounce) container sour cream

1 tablespoon lemon juice

1 tablespoon chopped fresh basil

1/2 teaspoon garlic salt

1/2 teaspoon black pepper

1 head iceberg lettuce, washed and torn into pieces

1 pound sliced bacon, cooked and crumbled

6 Roma tomatoes, thinly sliced

3 cups plain croutons

This dressing can be the star of a salad and doesn't need to be crowded out of the spotlight with loads of chopped vegetable additions. So use it alone over a simple mixture of mesclun salad greens or Bibb leaves.

୧୧

In a blender, combine the peaches, nectar, shallots, vinegar, salt, and pepper. Process until smooth. With the blender running, slowly add the oil in a steady stream until emulsified. Cover and refrigerate until ready to use.

# Fresh Peach Vinaigrette

**Makes about 2 cups**

3 large fresh peaches, peeled, pitted, and sliced

1/2 cup peach nectar

1 shallot, peeled and minced

1/4 cup cider vinegar

3/4 teaspoon salt

1/2 teaspoon ground white pepper

1/2 cup canola oil

# Eggplant and Sweet Onion Salad

**Makes 4 servings**

1 large eggplant

1 medium sweet onion, peeled and chopped

2 large tomatoes, chopped

4 tablespoons white wine vinegar

1 tablespoon olive oil

2 garlic cloves, minced

$1/2$ teaspoon salt

$1/4$ teaspoon cayenne pepper

Bibb or baby spinach leaves

Green onions for garnish, green parts only

**Broiling the eggplant softens it to a velvety texture, mellows out the flavor, and allows the sweet onions to shine. I like to serve this salad with short ribs.**

Preheat the broiler and place the rack in the center of the oven. Place the eggplant on a baking sheet and broil 15 to 20 minutes, turning every 5 minutes. Use a pick or tester to make sure the eggplant is soft all the way through. Set aside to cool.

Meanwhile, in a large bowl, stir together the onions and tomatoes. In a small jar with a tight-fitting lid, combine the vinegar, oil, garlic, salt, and cayenne. Shake well to emulsify. Pour over the tomato mixture.

Remove the skin from the eggplant and discard. Coarsely chop the eggplant. Toss gently with the tomato mixture. Cover and let stand at room temperature 15 minutes. Serve on a bed of greens, garnished with a sprinkling of chopped green onion tops.

**Note:** The salad can also be chilled and served cold.

I never have trouble getting my husband to have a salad for dinner if I make this meal. I like to make the dressing at the last minute and toss it with the greens just before serving. The leaves wilt slightly. Serve it with slices of hot cornbread to sop up the extra dressing.

# Hot Bacon Dressing over Wilted Greens

**Makes 6 to 8 servings**

4 bacon slices
2 tablespoons cider vinegar
2 tablespoons water
1 tablespoon sugar
1 egg, lightly beaten
Baby spinach leaves, room temperature

In a large skillet over medium heat, cook the bacon until crisp, about 8 minutes. Drain on paper towels and crumble when cool enough to handle.

Add the vinegar, water, and sugar to the drippings and bring to a boil. Remove from the heat and gradually stir a couple of tablespoons of the hot mixture into the beaten egg. Add the egg mixture to the skillet and reduce the heat to low. Stirring constantly, cook until thickened, around 3 minutes. Stir in the bacon.

Place the baby spinach on room temperature or slightly warmed salad plates. Drizzle the warm dressing generously over the top and serve immediately.

**Stoney Hollow Farm**

Scott and Stephanie Boxberger
944 Ollie's Creek Road
Robbinsville, North Carolina 28771
(828) 735-2983
E-mail: scott@stoneyhollowfarm.net
Website: www.stoneyhollowfarm.net
Consumer Experience: Pick your own, general store,
and vacation rental

*H*ave you ever harvested lettuce that was being grown in a greenhouse? If not, you won't believe how fun it is. Why? Because lettuce varieties tend to hit the market in the South before the weather wraps us all in a humid, summer-heated blanket. So to combat the persnickety spring weather that can range from chilly and damp to sometimes downright cold, greenhouse growing is the way to go.

That's why a trip to see Scott and Stephanie Boxberger at Stoney Hollow Farm needs to be on your springtime list of things to do. Their farm is located on the edge of the Great Smoky Mountains, so turn it into an early vacation while you're at it.

I immediately head toward the arugula, a peppery salad green that you can practically smell as soon as you hit the greenhouse door because it's so aromatic. I love the slightly hot, mustardy flavor it gives to my salad bowl. It looks a lot like radish greens.

Then waltz over to the mesclun mix, which could be called salad potpourri. It's a mixture of very young greens, and the medley of flavors makes a simple oil and vinegar dressing sing. The salad assembly continues with plenty of oakleaf, butterhead, leaf lettuce, micro-greens, and stunning red and green romaines. You'll enjoy them in and as a wrap, and they quickly turn an ordinary BLT sandwich into a lunch masterpiece.

A quick visit to Stoney Hollow's website makes it easy to see what is ready for picking at the moment. Just click on the produce calendar and you'll get a complete rundown of the items that are currently at their prime for harvesting. Then, no matter what the weather is like outside, you can comfortably pick your own salad greens at your leisure.

The first time I had this robust vinaigrette, it was tossed over roasted fall vegetables. It is equally divine over a mixture of sturdy salad greens, but I love it drizzled over wedges of crisp iceberg lettuce. You will be surprised how many guests are transported to their youth with this presentation.

Preheat the oven to 400°F. Place the beets in a lightly greased jelly-roll pan and toss with 1 tablespoon of the oil. Bake 35 minutes or until tender. Cool at least 15 minutes.

In the bowl of a food processor, combine the beets, remaining oil, vinegar, salt, and pepper. Process until smooth. Pour through a fine mesh strainer and discard the solids. Refrigerate the vinaigrette for at least 20 minutes.

Place the lettuce wedges on cold salad plates. Drizzle with the dressing and serve immediately.

# Fresh Beet Vinaigrette over Iceberg Wedges

## Makes 8 servings

2 beets, trimmed, peeled, and cut in thin wedges

1/2 cup olive oil, divided

2 tablespoons white wine vinegar

1/2 teaspoon salt

1/4 teaspoon black pepper

1 head iceberg lettuce, washed and cut into 8 wedges

# Tomato Bread Salad

## Makes 6 servings

6 cups cubed day-old, good quality crusty bread, like ciabatta or sourdough

5 fresh tomatoes, peeled and cut into large dice

1 small sweet onion, peeled and julienned

4 ounces fresh mozzarella, diced

1/2 cup chopped fresh basil

1 small head iceberg or butter lettuce, rinsed and torn into pieces

2/3 cup olive oil

1/4 cup sherry vinegar

2 garlic cloves, minced

1/2 teaspoon kosher salt

1/2 teaspoon black pepper

**The beauty of this salad is that the tomatoes are peeled, so nothing interferes with the flavor of the dressing. You can also seed the tomatoes, if desired. The dressing is a classic vinaigrette, and the entire dish is simple to prepare ahead of time, leaving time for you to enjoy your own dinner party.**

Place the bread cubes in the bottom of a large bowl. Top with the tomatoes, onions, mozzarella, basil, and lettuce.

In a jar with a tight-fitting lid, combine the oil, vinegar, garlic, salt, and pepper. Shake well to emulsify, and pour over the salad. Toss well. Let stand at room temperature 1 hour before serving.

Cilantro leaves are used as herbs, and the dried seeds, coriander, are used as a spice. The leaves add a lime-like zest to this lovely salad, with a proper mix of heat from the fresh peppers. I also love the dressing sprinkled over fish tacos or with grilled chicken.

❧

In a blender, place the cilantro, sour cream, jalapeños, juice, dressing mix, paprika, and pepper. Blend until smooth.

Place the lettuce leaves on cold salad plates. Drizzle the dressing generously over the top and serve immediately.

**Note:** Use the dressing immediately or cover and refrigerate until ready to use. Shake well before serving.

# Hot Cilantro Dressing over Mesclun Greens

**Makes 8 servings**

1 cup loosely packed cilantro
1 cup sour cream
2 jalapeño peppers, seeded
2 tablespoons lime juice
4 teaspoons dry Ranch dressing mix
1/4 teaspoon paprika
1/4 teaspoon white pepper
Mesclun lettuce leaves

If you've never made croutons out of cornbread, get ready to start. Leftovers will instantly become an addictive snack.

❧

Preheat the oven to 450°F. Lightly grease an 8-inch square baking pan and set aside.

In a mixing bowl, combine the cornmeal, flour, baking soda, and salt. Make a well in the center and set aside.

In a small bowl, whisk together the buttermilk, egg, and butter. Stir into the cornmeal mixture just until moistened. Spread in the prepared pan. Bake 10 to 12 minutes or until lightly browned. Remove from the oven and place the pan on a wire rack. Cool to room temperature.

Preheat the oven to 350°F. Lightly grease a jelly-roll pan. Cut the cooled cornbread into 1/2-inch cubes. Arrange in a single layer in the prepared pan and spray the tops with cooking spray. Bake 12 to 15 minutes or until browned. Serve warm.

# Cornbread Croutons

**Makes about 3 cups**

1/2 cup plain cornmeal
1/2 cup all-purpose flour
1/2 teaspoon baking soda
1/4 teaspoon salt
1/2 cup buttermilk
1 egg
1 tablespoon unsalted butter, melted

# Blueberry Horseradish Vinaigrette

This is one of my favorite dressings to serve over baby spinach leaves from my garden. It requires nothing else but a sprinkling of toasted nuts. This dressing is sweet, punchy, and filled with herbs. Search out one of the flavored vinegars called for in the ingredients list, if for nothing else than to make this dressing repeatedly.

❧

Combine the blueberries, vinegar, mustard, horseradish, honey, shallots, marjoram, and thyme in a blender or food processor. Puree until smooth.

With the motor running, slowly drizzle in the pumpkin seed and canola oils. Season with the salt and pepper, adding more if necessary. Refrigerate until ready to use.

### Makes 1 cup

1/4 cup fresh blueberries

1/4 cup peach, pear, or white wine vinegar

1 tablespoon prepared mustard

1 tablespoon prepared horseradish

1 tablespoon honey

1 shallot, peeled and chopped

1/2 teaspoon dried marjoram

1/2 teaspoon dried thyme

1 tablespoon pumpkin seed or walnut oil

1/2 cup canola oil

1/4 teaspoon salt

1/4 teaspoon black pepper

# Spotlight: Blueberries

## Berry Sweet Orchards

Cliff and Susan Muller
5110 Brown Road
Ethel, Louisiana 70730
(225) 683-8584
Website: www.berrysweetorchards.com
Consumer Experience: Pick your own

There's something to be admired about being the first, and Berry Sweet Orchards holds the title of Louisiana's first certified organic pick-your-own blueberry farm. Cliff and Susan Muller have been operating this exquisite farm since 1990 and are considered blueberry experts by those of us who love these sweet little blue gems.

Drive north of Baton Rouge on Highway 19 and you'll come to the little town of Ethel, Louisiana. Covering two acres of countryside are more than 1,500 organically grown blueberry bushes that burst forth with fruit in June and July.

Blueberries could be the easiest fruit you will ever harvest. All you have to do is "tickle" the fruit with a little wiggle and the berries practically fall off the branches into your waiting bucket. (Those that cling to the bush are not ready to pick and are usually not completely blue.) In a matter of minutes, you've got half a bucketful. Don't worry if you haven't done it before. Cliff and Susan will show you how!

Cliff caught the farmer bug after tasting the homegrown blueberries of a friend. It wasn't long before he and Susan purchased 20 acres and were on their way to becoming famous for the sweetest blueberries around. They grow numerous varieties: Austin, Brightwell, Climax, Delite, Premier, Tifblue (my favorite), and Woodard.

In addition, they grow squash, melons, and heirloom tomatoes (the Sungolds will change your life!). So pack a cooler, lace up your tennis shoes, and head on over. You'll definitely find a thrill there on the Mullers' blueberry hills.

# Warm Fig Dressing on Parmesan Greens

I adore the sweet edge given to this dressing by dried figs. You will too. It is all the fanciness a simple green salad needs. The sprinkling of freshly shredded Parmesan cheese adds just enough salt to make the salad sing.

❧

In a heavy saucepan over high heat, combine the wine, figs, shallots, and garlic. Cook 5 minutes. Transfer to a food processor or blender and add the vinegar and oil. Process until smooth.

Return the mixture to the saucepan and place over medium-high heat. Stir in the salt and pepper and bring to a boil.

Meanwhile, place the salad greens in a large serving bowl. Toss the hot dressing over the greens and divide among the serving plates. Top evenly with the shredded Parmesan and serve warm.

## Makes 6 servings

1 1/2 cups dry red wine

2 dried figs, chopped

1 shallot, peeled and chopped

1 garlic clove, minced

2 tablespoons balsamic vinegar

1/3 cup olive oil

1/2 teaspoon salt

1/4 teaspoon black pepper

6 cups mixed salad greens or baby spinach

1/2 cup shredded Parmesan cheese

The grill marks created on this corn only add to the presentation. The dressing is a simple vinaigrette that is not heavily seasoned. As it should be, most of the flavor comes from the fresh vegetables. Serve it on fresh lettuce leaves of any kind.

~

Spray the corn lightly with cooking spray and grill over medium hot coals, turning often so they don't burn but lightly char, about 7 minutes. Let cool to room temperature. With a sharp knife, cut the kernels from the cobs into a large mixing bowl.

Add the garlic, onions, tomatoes, bell peppers, jalapeños, and cilantro, mixing well. In a small bowl, whisk together the oil and vinegar. Pour over the vegetables. Season with the salt and pepper. Toss well. Cover and refrigerate at least 2 hours. Bring to room temperature before serving on crisp lettuce leaves.

# Grilled Corn Salad

Makes 6 servings

5 ears sweet corn, husked and silked

3 garlic cloves, minced

1 purple onion, peeled and julienned

2 ripe tomatoes, seeded and diced

1 orange bell pepper, roasted, peeled, seeded, and diced

1 jalapeño, seeded and minced

2 teaspoons chopped cilantro

1/4 cup olive oil

2 tablespoons red wine vinegar

1/4 teaspoon salt

1/2 teaspoon black pepper

Lettuce leaves

# Dilled Crawfish Salad

This salad is exceptional and should be reserved for any type of special occasion. It is New Orleans on a salad plate! On any of our many hot days, it's a refreshing do-ahead salad. Serve it with baguettes seared on the grill.

❧

**Makes 4 servings**

4 tablespoons unsalted butter

1 tablespoon olive oil

$1/4$ cup diced onions

$1/4$ cup diced celery

$1/4$ cup diced carrots

1 pound peeled crawfish tails

2 tablespoons dry white wine

1 tablespoon brandy

1 bay leaf

$1/2$ teaspoon garlic salt

$1/4$ teaspoon white pepper

$1/4$ teaspoon dried thyme

$1/4$ teaspoon hot sauce

$1/2$ cup mayonnaise

1 tablespoon lemon juice

2 teaspoon dried dill

Lettuce leaves

Lemon wedges

In a large skillet over medium heat, melt the butter. As soon as it foams, add the oil, onions, celery, and carrots. Sauté 4 minutes or until tender. Add the crawfish, wine, brandy, bay leaf, garlic salt, pepper, and thyme. Simmer 4 minutes and stir in the hot sauce. Remove from the heat and allow to sit undisturbed for 1 minute. Drain well, discarding the liquid and bay leaf. Cover and chill 30 minutes.

Meanwhile in a small mixing bowl, combine the mayonnaise, lemon juice, and dill. Remove the crawfish mixture from the refrigerator and add the mayonnaise mixture. Toss lightly. Serve on lettuce leaves with a lemon wedge on the side.

### Kyle LeBlanc Crawfish Farm

Kyle LeBlanc
302 Saint Peter Street
Raceland, Louisiana 70394
(985) 226-6444
E-mail: kyle@crawdads.net
Website: www.crawdads.net
Consumer Experience: Purchase online,
purchase in retail outlets

*A* tradition throughout most of the Deep South is a spring or early summer crawfish boil. It's a great excuse to have a large party and is fairly inexpensive during those months because of peak supplies. But a lot of us don't live in an area where crawfish is harvested. That's when Kyle LeBlanc's Crawfish Farm enters the picture.

This family-owned and operated business is my favorite crawfish source. The crawfish are huge and delicious! It feels like the state of Louisiana has been plopped into my own kitchen and backyard.

These freshwater crustaceans are very closely related to lobster and are equally tasty. Kyle has been supplying

live and boiled crawfish, crawfish tails, and soft-shell frozen crawfish since 1990. He knows what he's doing and obviously knows where to harvest the best Louisiana has to offer. He primarily has red swamp, white river, spillway, and Belle River crawfish, and he can tell you the difference quickly and so that you immediately understand. That knowledge base makes it easy to see why Kyle is the number one shipper of live crawfish in the country and he does so year-round.

So don't despair if you are in need of a taste of Cajun country and don't have a trip planned to Louisiana anytime soon. It can be delivered to your own door, and all you need is a large pot of boiling water to have a feast.

Pair this vinegar with a really good olive oil and your ordinary green salad is about to get a face lift. The raspberries give it a magnificent ruby color and a flavor that is exceptional. This recipe makes a lot, so put the extra in clear decorative bottles and it will be a welcome hostess gift.

# Ruby Raspberry Vinegar

**Makes 5 cups**

3 cups raspberries

2 (17-ounce) bottles white wine vinegar or champagne vinegar

1 cup sugar

Combine the raspberries, vinegar, and sugar in a large saucepan over medium-high heat. Bring to a boil, cover, and reduce the heat to low. Simmer 10 minutes. Pour through a fine mesh strainer into hot, sterilized jars or bottles. Use the back of a wooden spoon to extract as much liquid as possible. Discard the pulp. Seal and store in the refrigerator.

# Cherry Rice Salad

### Makes 6 servings

1 (6.2-ounce) package long grain and wild rice mix

1/2 cup dried cherries

2 green onions, chopped

1 Granny Smith apple, peeled and diced

1 carrot, peeled and grated

1 celery stalk, chopped

1/3 cup white balsamic vinegar

1/4 cup olive oil

1/4 teaspoon salt

1/4 teaspoon black pepper

1/2 cup chopped pecans or walnuts, toasted

**This chilled rice salad has an especially festive feel to it. Maybe it's the addition of cherries and nuts. Resist the urge to serve it with any less than eight hours of refrigerator time. It only gets better when allowed to fully meld before being served. So remember, the longer it sits, the better it gets!**

Cook the rice according to the package directions. Set aside to cool at least 20 minutes.

Meanwhile, stir together the cherries, onions, apples, carrots, and celery in a large mixing bowl.

Place the vinegar, oil, salt, and pepper in a jar with a tight-fitting lid. Shake to emulsify.

Add the cooled rice to the cherry mixture. Blend well. Add the vinegar mixture and mix well. Cover and refrigerate at least 8 hours. Stir in the pecans just before serving.

# Candied Carrot Dressing with Bibb Lettuce

### Makes 10 servings

2 cups shredded carrots

1 cup sweetened condensed milk

1/4 cup confectioners' sugar

1 tablespoon lemon juice

1 tablespoon honey

1/2 teaspoon lemon pepper

1/8 teaspoon salt

Bibb lettuce greens

**You can also use this sweet dressing with any veggie sandwich. I like to use it as a dip with chicken wraps, fresh mushrooms, or of course, as a salad dressing.**

Place the carrots, milk, sugar, juice, honey, pepper, and salt in the bowl of a blender or food processor. Blend until smooth.

Arrange lettuce greens on cold salad plates. Drizzle with the dressing and serve immediately.

**Note:** Use the dressing immediately or transfer to a covered container and refrigerate up to 3 days.

Use this dressing on any green salad, but the mixture of different salad greens is terrific. Throw in some peppery arugula to really accent the buttermilk flavor. It is particularly nice on any salad featuring turkey or chicken.

∞

In a jar with a tight-fitting lid, combine the buttermilk, honey, chives, parsley, juice, and pepper. Cover and shake well to emulsify. Refrigerate until ready to use.

To serve, arrange the lettuce leaves on cold salad plates. Shake the dressing and drizzle over greens. Serve immediately.

**Note:** Use the dressing within 1 week, and keep leftovers refrigerated.

# Honeyed Buttermilk Dressing over Mixed Greens

**Makes 6 to 8 servings**

$1/3$ cup buttermilk

$1/3$ cup honey

2 tablespoons chopped fresh chives

1 tablespoon chopped fresh parsley

2 tablespoons lemon juice

$1/2$ teaspoon black pepper

Mixed lettuce leaves (butterhead, crisphead, leaf, iceberg, romaine)

The simplicity of this salad is especially nice, and it's a full meal, thanks to the crispy bacon and fresh mushrooms. I like to serve it as a main dish with hot cornbread or hot water cornbread.

∞

Place the spinach, bacon, mushrooms, and eggs in a large salad bowl. Toss gently and set aside.

Place the oil, vinegar, wine, soy sauce, mustard, sugar, salt, pepper, and curry powder in a jar with a tight-fitting lid. Cover and shake vigorously until blended. Pour over the spinach salad and toss until all ingredients are evenly coated. Serve immediately.

# Fresh Spinach and Bacon Salad

**Makes 4 main or 8 salad course servings**

1 pound fresh spinach leaves, washed and trimmed

$1/2$ pound bacon, cooked and crumbled

6 ounces fresh mushrooms, sliced

3 hard-cooked eggs, chopped

$2/3$ cup olive oil

$1/4$ cup red wine vinegar

2 tablespoons dry red wine

2 teaspoons soy sauce

1 teaspoon dry mustard

1 teaspoon sugar

$1/2$ teaspoon garlic salt

$1/2$ teaspoon black pepper

$1/4$ teaspoon curry powder

# Sides

Creamy Mashed Cauliflower

Sweet and Sour Coleslaw

Cherry Tomato Covered Dish Salad

Freckle-Faced Carrot Casserole

Spring Dream Sausage and Spinach

Twice as Nice Corn Casserole

Pan-Roasted Poblano Corn

Pickin' and Grinnin' Corn Casserole

Midsummer Corn Salad

Orange Hugged Carrots

Summer Breeze Carrot Soufflé

Lemon Steamed Green Beans

Coconut Corn Fritters

Hot Cheddar Corn

Carolina Creamed Mushrooms

"Don't Get Above Your Raisin'" Apple Dressing

Ya'll Come Pecan Brussels Sprouts

Fresh Baked Eggplant

Balsamic Grilled Eggplant

Sauced Parsnips

Garlic Spinach Sauté

Mixed Peppered Turnips

Vinegar-Splashed Bacon Butter Beans

Bacon and Rutabaga Soufflé

Florida Sunshine Glazed Rutabagas

Three-Vegetable Sauté

Tomatoes with Cornbread Stuffing

Crowder Pea Succotash

The Best Southern Hash Browns

Mashed Potato Patties

So Simple Mashed Sweet Potatoes

Yazoo City Potatoes and Cream

Black-Eyed Pea Stew with Rice Waffles

Pull-out-the-Best-China Herbed Squash

Squash Napoleons

Field Pea Fritters

Spring Tonic Spinach

Marinated Lima Beans

Setting Sun–Kissed Parsnips

Peanut Sautéed Green Beans

Individual Zucchini and Corn Soufflés

Pocketbook Zucchini

Sausage Cornbread Dressing

Grilled Mixed Pepper Kabobs

Parsnip and Tart Apple Puree

Blue Cheese and Bacon Coleslaw

# Creamy Mashed Cauliflower

**Makes 8 servings**

1 large head cauliflower, cut into florets

²/₃ cup chicken or vegetable stock

1 teaspoon dried tarragon

¹/₂ teaspoon dried chives

¹/₂ teaspoon salt

¹/₄ teaspoon black pepper

²/₃ cup half-and-half

**Serve this clever side dish as a substitute for mashed potatoes, or don't hesitate to combine the two! I like to mix together equal parts of mashed cauliflower with mashed potatoes for a side with some character.**

Place the cauliflower and stock in a Dutch oven. Cover and place over high heat. Steam 10 minutes or until the stock has nearly evaporated.

Transfer the cauliflower to a food processor. Add the tarragon, chives, salt, and pepper. With the processor running, add the half-and-half in a steady stream. Puree until smooth. Serve warm.

# Sweet and Sour Coleslaw

**Makes 8 servings**

1 head cabbage, shredded

¹/₂ cup sugar

¹/₄ cup honey

2 teaspoons firmly packed light brown sugar

1 tablespoon salt

1 teaspoon dry mustard

²/₃ cup vegetable oil

1 cup cider vinegar

1 teaspoon celery seeds

**This is a really nice combination of sweet and savory. I like to serve this with grilled flank steak and homemade rolls.**

Place the cabbage in a large bowl. Sprinkle with the sugar and drizzle with honey. Do not stir.

In a small saucepan over medium-high heat, combine the brown sugar, salt, dry mustard, oil, vinegar, and seeds. Bring to a boil and remove from the heat. Let cool 15 minutes. Pour over the coleslaw, mixing well. Cover and refrigerate at least 4 hours before serving.

## Fayetteville Farmers' Market

101 West Mountain Street
Fayetteville, Arkansas 72702
(479) 236-2910
E-mail: fayettevillefm@gmail.com
Website: www.fayettevillefarmersmarket.org
Open Tuesday, Thursday, and Saturday mornings (April through mid-November)
Consumer Experience: Farmers' Market

Heading downtown has always been fun for me . . . any downtown. It is interesting to see how cities began with a central business area while expanded areas and homes fan out from there. If you've never been to downtown Fayetteville, Arkansas, you need to put gas in the car and go. It's just lovely, and strolling around the Farmers' Market is a perfect way to spend a morning.

For nearly 40 years, the Farmers' Market has been putting locally grown food in the hands of visitors, and it shows no signs of slowing down. The atmosphere is addictive, with loads of fresh aromas, healthy plants and flowers, music, crafts, and fine art. I like to go on Saturdays, arriving early and staying until it closes in the early afternoon.

If there is any fresh produce you are craving, you're likely to find it at this market. With more than 60 vendors, you've got it all. I found fabulous salad greens, radishes, sugar peas, and heirloom tomatoes on my last visit. My one-stop shopping allowed me to have an incredible fresh salad that evening while far away from home. It will do the same for you, whether you are just passing through or are there for an extended vacation. Give it a day and the Fayetteville Farmers' Market will give you a fine local food experience.

# Cherry Tomato Covered Dish Salad

**If you are headed outdoors for any type of food event, this is the perfect make-ahead dish to take with you. You don't have to worry about keeping it cold because it is just as nice served at room temperature. It complements chicken very well.**

❧

In a large saucepan over medium-high heat, bring the stock to a boil. Stir in the couscous. Cover and set aside 5 minutes or until all the liquid is absorbed.

Meanwhile, heat the oil in a large skillet over medium-high heat. Add the tomatoes, garlic, and shallots. Sauté 3 minutes or until the tomatoes begin to soften. Stir in the basil, salt, and pepper.

Add to the couscous and toss to mix. Adjust the salt and pepper if necessary. Serve warm, at room temperature, or cold.

**Makes 6 servings**

3 cups chicken or vegetable stock

1 1/2 cups couscous

1 tablespoon olive oil

2 cups cherry tomatoes

2 garlic cloves, minced

1 shallot, peeled and minced

1 tablespoon chopped fresh basil

1/2 teaspoon salt

1/4 teaspoon black pepper

# Freckle-Faced Carrot Casserole

## Makes 8 servings

1 tablespoon unsalted butter

1 large purple onion, peeled and chopped

1 pound wild or button mushrooms, chopped

1 1/2 teaspoons salt

1 teaspoon dried basil

1 teaspoon dried thyme

4 garlic cloves, minced

1 pound carrots, peeled and shredded

3 cups soft breadcrumbs, divided

1 cup grated Cheddar cheese

3 eggs, beaten

1/4 teaspoon black pepper

**I serve this side dish with grilled fish of any kind. It's just the right amount of color to add to your plate. Using a food processor to shred the carrots will greatly cut down on the preparation time.**

Preheat the oven to 350°F. Lightly grease a 13 x 9-inch baking dish and set aside.

In a large skillet over medium heat, melt the butter. As soon as it foams, add the onions and sauté 5 minutes. Add the mushrooms, salt, basil, thyme, and garlic. Sauté 10 minutes longer.

In a large bowl, combine the carrots, 2 cups of the breadcrumbs, cheese, eggs, and pepper. Add the mushroom mixture, mixing well. Spread into the prepared dish and sprinkle the top evenly with the remaining breadcrumbs.

Bake 30 minutes, covered. Uncover and bake 15 minutes longer. Serve hot or warm.

**I love this dish that utilizes early spinach and peas from my garden. Things always taste better when you grow and harvest them yourself. Of course, George prefers the sweet Italian sausage and I want the hot, so to the table with hot sauce I go!**

꙳

In a large saucepan, heat the oil over medium-high heat. Add the sausage and cook about 10 minutes or until completely done. Crumble the sausage with a spatula as it cooks. Transfer with a slotted spoon to a plate lined with paper towels, leaving the drippings in the pan. Set aside.

Reduce the heat to medium and add the onions and garlic to the pan. Cover and cook 4 minutes. Add the orzo and cook 2 minutes longer. Stir in the stock. Cook, stirring constantly until the orzo is al dente and suspended in a thick broth, about 15 minutes.

Season with the salt and pepper. Add the sausage, spinach, peas, and cheese. Cook until the peas are heated and the spinach is wilted, about 5 minutes longer. Serve warm.

# Spring Dream Sausage and Spinach

## Makes 6 servings

2 tablespoons vegetable oil

1 pound sweet or hot Italian sausage, casings removed

1 white onion, peeled and coarsely chopped

1 garlic clove, minced

1 1/2 cups (10 ounces) orzo

4 cups chicken or vegetable stock

1/2 teaspoon salt

1/4 teaspoon black pepper

2 cups loosely packed baby spinach leaves

1 cup fresh or frozen baby peas (if frozen, do not thaw)

6 tablespoons shredded Parmesan cheese

# Twice as Nice Corn Casserole

**Makes 10 servings**

3 (15.5-ounce) cans white hominy, drained

2 1/2 cups whole kernel white sweet corn

1 (4.5-ounce) can chopped green chiles, drained

1 tablespoon cornstarch

1/2 teaspoon white pepper

1 (8-ounce) container sour cream

1 1/2 cups shredded Monterey Jack cheese

1 1/2 cups shredded Swiss cheese

1/2 teaspoon paprika

This side dish features the goodness of both white hominy and white kernel corn. This is a great dish to serve to those who think they don't like hominy. It swims between layers of melted cheese.

Preheat the oven to 350°F. Lightly grease an 11 x 7-inch baking dish and set aside.

In a large mixing bowl, toss together the hominy, corn, and chiles. In a separate bowl, combine the cornstarch, pepper, and sour cream. Gently add to the hominy mixture, stirring to evenly coat. Spoon half of the hominy mixture into the prepared dish.

In a separate bowl, combine the Monterey Jack and Swiss cheeses. Sprinkle half of the cheese mixture over the hominy. Top the cheese with the remaining hominy mixture.

Cover and bake 35 minutes. Sprinkle with the remaining cheese and the paprika. Uncover and bake 5 minutes longer. Serve warm.

**This recipe is spiced just right and quick as lightning to prepare. The peppers and seasonings pump up the sweetness of the fresh corn.**

In a large skillet over medium heat, melt 6 tablespoons of the butter. As soon as the butter foams, add the corn and onions. Cook 5 minutes or until the onions are just beginning to brown.

Stir in the Creole seasoning, poblanos, and pepper. Cook 5 minutes. Add the remaining butter, stirring just until completely melted. Serve warm.

# Pan-Roasted Poblano Corn

**Makes 6 servings**

1/2 cup (1 stick) unsalted butter, divided

5 cups whole kernel sweet corn

1/2 cup chopped yellow onions

2 tablespoons Creole seasoning

1 fresh poblano pepper, seeded and chopped

1/4 teaspoon black pepper

83

# Pickin' and Grinnin' Corn Casserole

**Makes 10 servings**

1/2 cup (1 stick) unsalted butter
1/2 cup sour cream
2 eggs, lightly beaten
1 (6-ounce) package cornbread mix
2 (14.75-ounce) cans cream-style corn
2 cups fresh whole kernel sweet corn
1/2 teaspoon garlic powder
1/2 teaspoon white pepper
1/2 cup crushed butter crackers

**There are quite literally dozens of versions of this family classic. This one happens to be the recipe I use over and over, especially for my friend Laura's birthday party. It's her request, and the guests are always grateful.**

Preheat the oven to 350°F. Place the butter in a 13 x 9-inch baking dish to melt while the oven preheats.

Meanwhile, in a large mixing bowl, whisk together the sour cream and eggs. Add the cornbread mix and cream-style corn, mixing well. Stir in the whole kernel corn, garlic powder, and pepper. Pour onto the melted butter and do not stir.

Sprinkle the top with the crushed crackers and bake 1 hour. Let stand 5 minutes before serving.

# Midsummer Corn Salad

**Makes 6 servings**

1 tablespoon olive oil
3 cups whole kernel sweet corn
1 cup fresh baby lima beans
1/4 cup diced roasted red bell pepper
1 tablespoon julienned fresh basil leaves
1 tablespoon lemon juice
3/4 teaspoon salt
1/4 teaspoon crushed red pepper

**This salad is perfect when you have both corn and lima beans ready to pick in the garden or after a trip to the fresh market or local farm in your community. Make it ahead and just pull it out of the refrigerator 20 minutes before serving time.**

Place the oil in a large skillet over medium-high heat. When hot, add the corn and beans. Sauté 5 minutes or until the vegetables are tender. Let cool at least 10 minutes.

Stir in the peppers, basil, lemon juice, salt, and red pepper. Cover and refrigerate at least 1 hour before serving. Serve at room temperature.

This versatile side dish is quick and super easy. It is nice with any meat that is roasted or grilled, but particularly complements chicken or pork.

In a medium saucepan over medium heat, cook the carrots in 1/2 cup of water for 5 minutes or until the desired doneness is reached. Drain and add the butter. Set aside.

In a small bowl, whisk together the juice, cornstarch, sugar, salt, and ginger. Pour over the hot carrots and toss well to evenly coat. Serve warm.

# Orange Hugged Carrots

**Makes 4 servings**

1 pound carrots, peeled and cut into diagonal 1/2-inch slices

1 tablespoon unsalted butter

1/4 cup orange juice

2 tablespoons cornstarch

1 tablespoon sugar

1/2 teaspoon salt

1/4 teaspoon ground ginger

# Summer Breeze Carrot Soufflé

### Makes 6 servings

1 1/2 pounds carrots, peeled and sliced
12 tablespoons (1 1/2 sticks) unsalted butter
3 eggs, separated
1/4 cup all-purpose flour
1 1/2 teaspoons baking powder
1 1/2 cups sugar
1/8 teaspoon ground nutmeg or cinnamon

**Resist the urge to open the oven door for a peek at your creation. The sudden drop in temperature can cause the soufflé to fall. If you have to see it, turn on the oven light and look through the glass. Have the rest of the meal ready so you can serve this straight from the oven. It is beyond great for brunch.**

Place the carrots in a medium saucepan and barely cover with water. Bring to a boil over high heat and cook 10 minutes. Drain well.

Meanwhile preheat the oven to 350°F. Lightly grease a 1 1/2-quart soufflé dish and set aside.

Place the carrots, butter, eggs, flour, baking powder, sugar, and nutmeg in the bowl of a food processor. Process until smooth. Transfer to the prepared dish and bake 1 hour or until set and lightly browned. Serve immediately.

# Lemon Steamed Green Beans

### Makes 8 servings

2 pounds fresh green beans, trimmed
2/3 cup vegetable or chicken stock
2 tablespoons olive oil
1/2 teaspoon salt
1/4 teaspoon black pepper
1 tablespoon grated lemon zest
1 lemon, cut into 8 wedges

**This recipe marries pan frying and steaming, giving the beans a nice crisp yet tender texture. This is not your ordinary, cooked-to-death side dish of Southern green beans. Each guest has a lemon wedge to personally adjust the amount of citrusy flavor they prefer.**

Place the beans in a large skillet. In a small bowl, whisk together the stock, oil, salt, and pepper. Pour over the beans. Cover and place over high heat. When the beans begin to steam, cook 7 to 8 minutes or until all the liquid evaporates. Stir in the zest and serve warm with lemon wedges.

**Note:** If you like things really hot, substitute cayenne for the black pepper.

## Gallrein Farms

Bill Gallrein
1029 Vigo Road
Shelbyville, Kentucky 40065
(502) 633-4849
E-mail: gallreinfarms@aol.com
Website: www.gallreinfarms.com
Consumer Experience: Farm market, petting zoo

*B*eginning in late June and running through October, Gallrein Farms in Shelbyville, Kentucky, becomes a green bean mecca. There is something incredibly hypnotic about watching mechanical harvesters work a bean field. I truly believe I could sit and watch for hours. It's so America!

Bill Gallrein is known for his green beans throughout Kentucky and beyond. He is considered a premier producer, and if it's for sale in his market, you know you are getting the best. In addition to green beans, you'll find bins overflowing throughout the summer months with sweet corn, tomatoes, okra, potatoes, and squash, freshly picked each day from his picture-perfect farm.

There are plenty of things to do at Gallrein Farms to educate young minds about farm life. The petting zoo is always full of kids anxious to feed, hold, stroke, and just look at the animals. Crowd favorites are Patrick, the miniature horse, and Eeyore, the Sicilian donkey, but you'll also find goats, pigs, sheep, calves, ducks, geese, and a llama, as well as a catfish pond. You'll be surprised how relaxing the environment is, and you'll come away with the finest green beans ever grown.

# Coconut Corn Fritters

**Makes 8 servings**

1/2 cup vegetable or canola oil
2 cups whole kernel sweet corn
1/4 cup all-purpose flour
1 egg, lightly beaten
3 garlic cloves, minced
2 tablespoons coconut milk
1 teaspoon salt
1/4 teaspoon white pepper

These "dressed-up" fritters use coconut milk to add a hint of sweetness. Just a bit makes a huge difference in the recipe. Refrigerate the leftover portion for other uses. I like to serve these with any type of grilled fish or chicken.

❧

Heat the oil in a large skillet over medium-high heat.

Meanwhile, in a large bowl, combine the corn, flour, egg, garlic, coconut milk, salt, and pepper. Stir well.

When the oil is hot, carefully drop in the fritter batter by heaping tablespoons into the skillet. Be careful not to overcrowd the pan. Fry until golden brown on one side, about 2 minutes. Flip and fry until completely golden brown, around 1 minute longer. Drain on paper towels and repeat with the remaining batter. Serve warm.

# Hot Cheddar Corn

**Makes 6 to 8 servings**

2 cups whole kernel sweet corn
4 eggs, lightly beaten
3/4 cup plain cornmeal
1 tablespoon baking powder
1/2 teaspoon salt
1/2 cup bacon drippings (or 1 stick melted unsalted butter)
3 jalapeños, seeded and finely chopped
1 cup shredded Cheddar cheese

You could use field corn for this recipe, but I prefer sweet because of the extra creaminess it gives the end product. This recipe is a reason to save bacon drippings. Pour them into a container and refrigerate until ready to use. Then melt on low power in the microwave in order to measure for recipes.

❧

Preheat the oven to 350°F. Lightly grease a 2-quart baking dish and set aside.

In a large mixing bowl, combine the corn and eggs. Add the cornmeal, baking powder, salt, bacon drippings, and jalapeños. Mix well and fold in the cheese. Pour into the prepared dish and bake 45 minutes or until the top is golden brown. Serve warm.

# Spotlight: Corn

## Mitchell Farms

Dennis and Nelda Mitchell
650 Leaf River Church Road
Collins, Mississippi 39428
(601) 765-8609
Website: www.mitchellfarms-ms.com
Consumer Experience: Farm market, cabin tours

Mississippi is famous for a lot of things: heat, humidity, the namesake mighty river—oh, and sweet corn! Perhaps it's that combination of heat and humidity that helps the annual corn crop taste so sugary. Whatever it is, I am ready for it as soon as the temperature upturns to nearly unbearable.

Drive southeast from the capital city of Jackson, and before you reach Hattiesburg, you'll come to a town named Collins. Anyone you encounter from the city limits on will be able to direct you to Mitchell Farms. You don't even have to say the name of the farm! Just ask how to find Dennis and Nelda.

After farming soybeans for years, this adorable couple decided to diversify into a farm that offers both you-pick items and already-picked vegetables. That's where the sweet corn comes in. According to Dennis, few can correctly pick sweet corn without tearing up the stalks of the plant. Therefore, he offers sweet corn, summer squash, and cucumbers that are harvested daily for customer convenience beginning in June and continuing through the summer. The sweet corn is blessed with sugar-filled kernels from the silky top to the bottom. It is "let me eat this now" good, and my freezer supply keeps me corn happy all winter long.

The old-fashioned cabins throughout the property will charm you. It is a field trip for adults and children alike who want a glimpse into the life of days gone by. They provide a realistic view of how farming life was in the not-so-distant past, and you'll appreciate the attention to detail found in each one.

So, thanks, Dennis and Nelda, for treating us to a great, educational on-farm experience. You can tell they love both the harvest and the land. As Dennis told me, "This beats the peep out of soybean farming!"

# Carolina Creamed Mushrooms

There are times when I serve this incredibly creamy dish on simple toasted loaf bread. Then I may enjoy it the next time with roast beef. It is robust and filling either way. The mushrooms bubble away in a creamy cheese sauce and are topped with chunky toasted bread crumbs.

❧

**Makes 8 servings**

1 (10-ounce) package frozen spinach, thawed

4 tablespoons olive oil, divided

1 pound button or cremini mushrooms, cut in half lengthwise

2 tablespoons lemon juice

2 tablespoons sliced green onions

2 teaspoons dried parsley

1 garlic clove, minced

1/2 teaspoon salt

1/4 teaspoon black pepper

2 tablespoons red wine

4 ounces cream cheese, room temperature

1 cup sour cream, room temperature

3 ounces crumbled feta cheese

3 slices toasted bread, crumbled

Between paper towels, squeeze the excess moisture out of the spinach and set aside. Preheat the oven to 350°F. Lightly grease a 2-quart baking dish and set aside.

Place 2 tablespoons of the oil in a large skillet over medium heat. Add the mushrooms and cook 3 minutes. Add the lemon juice, onions, parsley, garlic, salt, and pepper. Cook 3 minutes more, stirring often.

Add the wine and reduce 4 minutes. Add the cream cheese and stir until melted. Gradually add the sour cream, feta, and spinach, blending well. Spoon into the prepared baking dish.

Place the remaining oil in the skillet. Add the breadcrumbs and stir-fry until golden, about 4 minutes. Sprinkle over the mushroom mixture. Bake 30 minutes or until hot and bubbly. Cool 5 minutes before serving.

**Tart, fresh apples are combined with dried apples and golden raisins to lift this dressing to scrumptious. Serve this fruit-filled dressing with roasted turkey or pork. It tastes like fall no matter when you serve it.**

❧

Heat the oil in a large skillet over medium heat. Add the onions and garlic. Sauté 5 minutes or until the onions are translucent.

Add the fresh apples and cook 4 minutes longer. Add the dried apples, raisins, sage, and breadcrumbs, stirring to combine. Add the cider and increase the heat to medium-high. Cook 5 minutes, stirring occasionally. Remove from the heat and season with the salt and pepper. Serve hot or warm.

**Note:** To make soft breadcrumbs, simply put a few slices of bread in a food processor and give it a whirl.

# "Don't Get Above Your Raisin'" Apple Dressing

**Makes 6 to 8 servings**

2 tablespoons olive oil

1 1/2 cups finely chopped yellow onions

2 garlic cloves, minced

2 Newtown Pippin or Granny Smith apples, peeled, cored, and chopped

1 cup chopped dried apples

1/3 cup golden raisins

1 tablespoon chopped fresh sage

1/2 cup soft breadcrumbs

1 cup apple cider

1/4 teaspoon salt

1/4 teaspoon black pepper

This is the dish to use for transforming Brussels sprouts detractors you might know. It goes well with roasted turkey. The pecans add just a bit of crunch to these baby members of the cabbage family.

❧

Place the bacon in a Dutch oven over medium-high heat. Cook about 6 minutes, stirring frequently, until nearly crisp. Add the garlic and cook 1 minute longer. Remove with a slotted spoon onto paper towels to drain, and set aside.

In the same pot, add the Brussels sprouts, water, butter, sugar, salt, and pepper. Simmer 15 minutes, stirring occasionally. Add the reserved bacon and garlic, and the pecans. Cook 2 minutes and serve warm.

# Y'all Come Pecan Brussels Sprouts

**Makes 8 servings**

6 thick bacon slices, cut into $1/2$-inch pieces

2 garlic cloves, minced

3 pounds fresh Brussels sprouts, trimmed and cut in half

1 $1/2$ cups water

2 tablespoons unsalted butter

1 teaspoon sugar

$1/2$ teaspoon kosher salt

$1/4$ teaspoon white pepper

1 cup chopped pecans, toasted

# Fresh Baked Eggplant

**Butter-tender eggplant is enhanced with fresh tomatoes and cheese in this side dish. Serve it with grilled or roasted meat or poultry.**

### Makes 6 servings

1 tablespoon unsalted butter, softened
1 pound eggplant, peeled, halved, and cut into 1/2-inch slices
1/2 teaspoon kosher salt
1/4 teaspoon black pepper
3 tomatoes, peeled, seeded, and chopped
1/2 cup shredded Swiss cheese

Preheat the oven to 350°F. Place the butter in a 2-quart shallow baking dish and place in the preheating oven to melt. When melted, arrange the eggplant slices in the dish so they slightly overlap. Sprinkle evenly with the salt and pepper. Spread the tomatoes evenly over the eggplant. Top with the cheese.

Bake 25 to 30 minutes or until the eggplant is tender when pierced with a fork. Let stand 10 minutes before serving.

**Tip:** If you're looking for an easier way to peel eggplant, put down the paring knife and pick up the vegetable peeler.

# Balsamic Grilled Eggplant

**A plate of grilled eggplant becomes a feast when you drizzle it with balsamic vinegar. Use a really good aged vinegar for this dish since it's the main seasoning. Invest in the best you can afford, and save it for recipes like this one.**

### Makes 4 servings

1 large eggplant
2 tablespoons olive oil
1/2 teaspoon kosher salt
2 tablespoons balsamic vinegar

Preheat the grill to medium (350°F).

Meanwhile, cut the eggplant horizontally into 4 large pieces. Brush the cut edges with the oil and sprinkle with the salt. Grill 8 minutes on each side or until tender. Brush with the vinegar and serve warm.

## Ballston Farmers' Market

Wellburn Square (North Stuart & North Ninth Street)
Arlington, Virginia 22201
(703) 528-0311
E-mail: Jessica@iloveballston.com
Website: www.iloveballston.com
Open Thursdays from 3:00 to 7:00 p.m.
(End of May through mid-October)
Consumer Experience: Farmers' market

*I* like to begin preparing for my weekend on Thursdays. That's why I love the Ballston Farmers' Market, an outdoor facility open every Thursday at 3:00 p.m. from the end of May through the middle of October. After work, you can stop by to pick up anything and everything—and I mean *every*thing!—you need for upcoming weekend festivities.

This is a true farmers' market, where each vendor brings his or her own tent, tables, and signs. As you walk through the market, you have all kinds of freshness in front of you. The market has a unique "producer only rule," which means you will be purchasing directly from the person who grew or produced what you see. Products must come from within a 200-mile radius of Arlington, so this is wonderfully local food.

I am particularly fond of the fresh herbs and produce, but don't think you'll be limited to just those items. Ballston Farmers' Market offers exceptional artisan breads, pound cakes, cupcakes, truffles, chocolates, teas, and premium roasted coffees. Don't leave without a famous whoopie pie. It is mad good! Plus, enjoy tunes from local musicians as you shop. Every visit to Ballston puts you in the mind-set for a fabulous weekend.

# Sauced Parsnips

**Parsnips puree beautifully after being cooked. These are sauced up a bit with wine, cream, and butter. It is divine with any wild game.**

❧

Fill a large Dutch oven with water and bring to a boil over medium-high heat. Add the parsnips and cover. Boil 20 minutes or until they are tender and easily pierced with a fork.

Meanwhile, preheat the oven to 375°F. Lightly grease a 6-cup baking dish and set aside.

Drain the parsnips and transfer to a food processor or blender. Add 6 tablespoons of the butter, wine, cream, nutmeg, and salt. Process until smooth.

Transfer to the prepared baking dish. Sprinkle the pecans evenly over the top and dot with the remaining 2 tablespoons of butter. Bake 20 minutes or until bubbly. Serve hot.

### Makes 8 servings

5 pounds parsnips, peeled

1/2 cup (1 stick) unsalted butter, softened and divided

1/2 cup dry red wine

1/4 cup cream

1/4 teaspoon ground nutmeg

1/4 teaspoon salt

2/3 cup chopped pecans or walnuts

# Garlic Spinach Sauté

**This is one of my favorite spinach side dishes. The leaves wilt quickly in garlicky hot oil, so the heaping leaves when fresh reduce quickly to serve just two. I like to serve it as a side with pork or chicken.**

❧

Heat the oil in a large skillet over medium-high heat. Add the garlic and sauté 30 seconds. Add the spinach and cook 4 minutes or until the spinach is wilted. Sprinkle with the salt and pepper and serve immediately with tongs or a slotted spoon.

### Makes 2 servings

1 teaspoon olive oil

1 garlic clove, minced

2 cups fresh spinach leaves

1/4 teaspoon kosher salt

1/4 teaspoon black pepper

Southerners have long mixed turnips and potatoes together in the same cooking pot. You'll see why with one taste of this side dish. Turnips are easy to grow and even easier to keep. You can refrigerate them, but a cool, dry cellar or basement is best. If you don't have bacon drippings, you can easily substitute vegetable or canola oil.

❧

Combine the turnips, potatoes, bay leaf, and stock in a large Dutch oven over medium-high heat. Bring to a boil, cover, and reduce the heat to medium-low. Simmer 20 minutes or until the vegetables are tender.

Meanwhile, place the drippings in a medium skillet over medium heat. Add the onions and sauté 5 minutes, stirring frequently.

Drain the turnip mixture and discard the bay leaf. Transfer to a serving bowl. Add the onions and pan drippings, tossing gently. Sprinkle with the salt, pepper, cayenne, and parsley. Toss slightly and serve warm.

# Mixed Peppered Turnips

**Makes 8 servings**

2 pounds turnips, peeled and cubed

2 new potatoes, unpeeled and cubed

1 bay leaf

4 cups vegetable stock or water

2 tablespoons bacon drippings

1 white onion, peeled and chopped

1/2 teaspoon kosher salt

1/2 teaspoon black pepper

1/4 teaspoon cayenne pepper

1 tablespoon chopped fresh parsley

A really good, high-quality balsamic vinegar that's been aged for at least ten years is necessary for this recipe. It only uses a little, but it makes the butter beans sing!

❧

Place the beans in a large saucepan and cover with water. Bring to a boil over medium-high heat. Reduce the heat to low and simmer 30 minutes, stirring occasionally. Drain and set aside.

Meanwhile, fry the bacon in a large skillet over medium-high heat until crisp, around 8 minutes. Remove with a slotted spoon and drain on paper towels. Add the onions and garlic to the skillet drippings and cook 2 minutes longer.

Add the beans, parsley, salt, and pepper. Cook 1 minute. Splash the vinegar over the top and cook 1 minute longer. Crumble the bacon and sprinkle over the top. Serve warm.

# Vinegar–Splashed Bacon Butter Beans

**Makes 6 servings**

2 1/2 cups fresh butter beans

6 slices bacon

4 green onions, chopped

2 garlic cloves, minced

1/2 cup chopped fresh parsley

1/2 teaspoon seasoned salt

1/2 teaspoon black pepper

1 tablespoon balsamic vinegar

# Bacon and Rutabaga Soufflé

Salty bacon pairs beautifully with ever-so-slightly sweet rutabagas to make this warm side dish unforgettable. Rutabagas are the warm-season members of the cabbage family. If desired, you can substitute peeled and sliced turnips for the rutabagas.

**Makes 8 servings**

1 rutabaga, peeled and cut in 1/2-inch slices

1 1/2 teaspoons salt, divided

1/2 cup (1 stick) unsalted butter

2 tablespoons all-purpose flour

2/3 cup milk

4 eggs, separated

4 bacon slices, cooked and crumbled

Place the rutabagas in a Dutch oven and sprinkle with 1/2 teaspoon of the salt. Cover with water and place over medium-high heat. Cook 45 minutes or until tender. Drain well and transfer to a mixing bowl. Using an electric mixer, beat at low speed until smooth.

Preheat the oven to 350°F. Lightly grease an 11 x 7-inch baking dish and set aside.

Place the butter in the Dutch oven and place over medium heat. When the butter has completely melted and begins to foam, whisk in the flour and the remaining salt. Cook 1 minute, whisking constantly to cook off the starchy flavor. Gradually stir in the milk. Cook 2 minutes, whisking constantly.

Beat the egg yolks in a small bowl. Gradually add 1/2 cup of the milk mixture to the eggs, whisking to combine. Add to the remaining milk mixture in the pot and blend well. Stir in the rutabagas and remove from the heat. Set aside.

With an electric mixer, beat the egg whites at medium-high speed until stiff peaks form. Fold into the rutabaga mixture and transfer to the prepared pan. Sprinkle the top evenly with the bacon. Bake 40 minutes or until golden brown. Serve immediately.

# Florida Sunshine Glazed Rutabagas

Sunny lemons give this carrot and rutabaga combination zip. The pale yellow flesh is highlighted by the orange, making it great to serve with a bland-colored main dish. I like to pair this with fish.

**Makes 4 servings**

1/2 rutabaga, peeled and cut in thin strips
6 carrots, peeled and cut in thin strips
1 cup water
2 tablespoons unsalted butter
1 tablespoon brown sugar
1/2 teaspoon grated lemon zest
1 tablespoon fresh lemon juice
1/4 teaspoon salt
1/4 teaspoon chopped fresh dill

Place the rutabagas, carrots, and water in a heavy saucepan over medium-high heat. Bring to a boil, cover, and reduce the heat to medium-low. Simmer 15 minutes. Drain the vegetables, remove the vegetables to a bowl, and set aside.

Using the same saucepan in which the vegetables were cooked, melt the butter over medium heat. Add the sugar, zest, juice, salt, and dill.

Return the vegetable mixture to the saucepan and gently toss with the lemon mixture. Cook 2 minutes, stirring frequently. Serve warm.

99

# Three-Vegetable Sauté

Yellow rutabagas, white turnips, and green broccoli team up in this gorgeous mixture of flavors and colors. The vegetables can be blanched up to 2 hours ahead of serving time, with the sautéing being done at the last minute. Serve this bright and flavorful side dish with roasted meat of any kind.

❧

**Makes 6 servings**

1 1/2 teaspoons salt, divided
1 rutabaga, peeled and thinly sliced
2 turnips, peeled and thinly sliced
Stems from 1 bunch of broccoli, thinly sliced into matchsticks (save the florets for another use)
6 tablespoons unsalted butter
1/4 teaspoon black pepper

Add one teaspoon of the salt to a large saucepan of water and place over medium-high heat. When the water comes to a boil, add the rutabagas, turnips, and broccoli slices. Cook 2 minutes and drain well. Immediately plunge into ice water and leave for 1 minute. Drain well and pat dry on paper towels.

In a heavy skillet with a lid, melt the butter over medium-high heat. Add the vegetable mixture to the butter, cover, and cook 2 minutes. Season with the remaining salt and the pepper. Cook 2 minutes longer. Serve warm.

# Tomatoes with Cornbread Stuffing

After I've had my fill of tomato sandwiches, I like to stuff tomatoes with this cornbread mixture and serve them as a nice light lunch. It works best with the largest tomatoes you can find. Serve on crisp lettuce leaves for a complete meal.

❧

**Makes 6 servings**

6 firm ripe tomatoes
1 recipe Paprika Cornbread (page 141), cooked, cooled, and crumbled
6 slices bacon, cooked and crumbled
4 green onions, chopped
1/4 cup mayonnaise
1/4 teaspoon salt
1/4 teaspoon black pepper
1/4 cup grated Parmesan cheese

Preheat the oven to 375°F. Lightly grease a 13 x 9-inch baking dish and set aside.

Cut a 1/4-inch slice from the top of each tomato. Scoop the pulp into a large mixing bowl, leaving the shells intact. Place the shells upside down on paper towels to drain at least 20 minutes.

Add the cornbread, bacon, onions, mayonnaise, salt, and pepper to the tomato pulp. Mix well and spoon into the tomato shells, packing tightly. Place on the prepared pan and sprinkle with the cheese.

Bake 15 minutes or until thoroughly heated. Serve warm.

**Who says lima beans always have to hold the succotash spotlight? Not me! The word *succotash* comes from the Indian word that means "boiled whole kernels of *corn*."**

⁓

Place the oil in a large skillet over medium heat. When hot, add the yellow onions, green peppers, and red peppers. Sauté 6 to 7 minutes or until very tender. Stir in the corn and peas. Cook 1 minute longer.

Add the cooking liquid, green onions, thyme, salt, and pepper. Cook 3 minutes or until heated through. Serve warm.

# Crowder Pea Succotash

**Makes 8 servings**

3 tablespoons olive oil

1 small yellow onion, peeled and chopped

1 green bell pepper, seeded and chopped

1 red bell pepper, seeded and chopped

2 cups whole kernel sweet corn

2 cups cooked crowder peas

1/2 cup reserved crowder pea cooking liquid or vegetable stock

1/2 cup sliced green onions

1 tablespoon chopped fresh thyme

1/2 teaspoon kosher salt

1/4 teaspoon black pepper

**Although typically served for weekend breakfasts, these transition well to any meal, especially when you want to have breakfast for dinner.**

⁓

Fill a large saucepan or Dutch oven with water and bring to a boil over high heat. Add the potatoes and cook 10 minutes, uncovered. Drain well and refrigerate 30 minutes. Dice the potatoes and set aside.

In a large cast iron skillet over medium-high heat, melt the drippings and butter, stirring to blend. Add the potatoes, stirring gently. Cook 10 minutes, turning occasionally.

Add the garlic, salt, and pepper, stirring gently. Cook 10 minutes longer or until the potatoes are golden brown on all sides. Serve warm.

# The Best Southern Hash Browns

**Makes 4 servings**

4 medium red potatoes, cut in half

2 tablespoons bacon drippings

2 tablespoons unsalted butter

2 garlic cloves, minced

1/4 teaspoon kosher salt

1/4 teaspoon black pepper

# Mashed Potato Patties

**Some people call these potato cakes, but I grew up calling them potato patties. They are the perfect way to used leftover mashed potatoes.**

⊷

### Makes 6 servings

1/2 cup vegetable or canola oil
2 cups mashed potatoes
1 cup shredded mozzarella cheese
2 eggs
1/2 teaspoon garlic salt
1/2 teaspoon onion powder
1/2 teaspoon black pepper
1 cup soft breadcrumbs

Heat the oil in a large cast iron skillet over medium heat.

Meanwhile, in a large bowl, combine the potatoes, cheese, 1 of the eggs, garlic salt, onion powder, and pepper, mixing well. Shape into 6 thick patties and set aside.

Place the remaining egg in a shallow dish and lightly beat. Place the breadcrumbs in a separate shallow dish. Dip each patty in the egg, then in the breadcrumbs.

Fry patties in the hot oil 10 to 12 minutes on each side or until golden brown. Drain on paper towels and serve warm.

**Note:** The patties can be shaped and refrigerated up to a day ahead. You can also completely make them up to 1 hour ahead of time. Let them stand loosely covered at room temperature and reheat in a 400°F oven for 5 minutes before serving.

# So Simple Mashed Sweet Potatoes

**There are times you don't want to fancy up sweet potatoes but really don't want to serve them just baked either. Here's where simplicity meets the road . . . deliciously!**

⊷

### Makes 4 servings

5 cups peeled, chopped sweet potatoes
2 tablespoons unsalted butter, softened
1 1/2 tablespoons honey
1 tablespoon milk
1/8 teaspoon ground cinnamon
1/8 teaspoon salt

Place the sweet potatoes in a large Dutch oven and cover with water. Place over medium-high heat and bring to a boil. Cover and reduce the heat to medium-low. Simmer 10 to 12 minutes or until the potatoes are tender. Drain and return to the Dutch oven to dry for 3 minutes.

Add the butter, honey, milk, cinnamon, and salt. Beat at medium speed with a hand mixer until smooth. Serve hot.

## Spotlight: Sweet Potato

### Hinton's Orchard & Farm Market

Jeremy and Joanna Hinton
8631 Campbellsville Road
Hodgenville, Kentucky 42748
(270) 325-3854
Website: www.hintonsorchard.com
Consumer Experience: Tour, farm market, bakery, playland

*A*lthough we see sweet potatoes on the market year-round, they are only available from local producers in the late summer through the fall months. That's a perfect time to head outside and one of the many reasons to head to Hodgenville, Kentucky. Their sweet potatoes are so sweet, no enhancement is needed after baking.

What began eight generations ago in the Hinton family with a farm of tobacco, hay, and grain has changed greatly over the years. Jeremy and Joanna Hinton began to diversify the family farm operation back in 2002 and renamed it Hinton's Orchard & Farm Market. Today, it is a family fun destination throughout the growing season.

Things kick off in the spring with strawberries and progress through peaches, apples, pumpkins, and delicious sweet potatoes. The Farmland play area is what sets this farm apart from others. Take, for instance, the grain bin. Traditionally used for storage, it now has been transformed into a playground for children, complete with toy dump trucks, tractors, and front-end loaders. Kids use the grain as a source of creative fun, and it's really hard not to get in and join them.

But the best time to go is in the fall. While you are digging through piles of sweet potatoes and harvesting pumpkins, don't miss the corn maze. It covers more than 3 acres, and guests go through over a mile of unique trails. It's a great way to enjoy a day out of doors and benefit from time on a true, working farm.

# Yazoo City Potatoes and Cream

I created this dish while I was in my first job out of college in Yazoo City, Mississippi. Potatoes fit into my tight budget just perfectly, and this dish would feed me at least half of the week. I like it to this day.

❧

## Makes 6 servings

4 medium white round potatoes, peeled and cut into thin slices

1/2 small white onion, peeled and cut into thin slices

5 tablespoons unsalted butter, divided

2 1/2 tablespoons all-purpose flour

3/4 teaspoon salt

1/2 teaspoon white pepper

2 cups heavy whipping cream

1/2 cup dry seasoned breadcrumbs

Preheat the oven to 300°F. Lightly grease a 2-quart baking dish and place a single layer of potatoes in the bottom of the dish. Top with a layer of the onions. Set aside the remaining potatoes and onions. You should have about a third of each remaining.

In a heavy saucepan over medium heat, melt 3 tablespoons of the butter. As soon as the butter foams, add the flour, salt, and pepper, whisking well. Cook 1 minute. Gradually add the cream and stir constantly until the sauce thickens, about 8 minutes.

Pour 1/4 cup of the sauce over the potatoes and onions in the prepared dish. Continue alternating single layers of the potatoes and onions, then covering with 1/4 cup sauce. Pour any extra sauce over the top.

In a small skillet, melt the remaining butter. Toss with the breadcrumbs to evenly coat. Sprinkle evenly over the top of the potatoes. Bake 30 minutes or until bubbly. Let stand 5 minutes before serving.

Because I tend to make a boatload when I cook peas, I always have leftovers. Much of that goes in the freezer for an easy, already-cooked side dish later, but 3 cups will forever get stashed away in the refrigerator for making this recipe the following night. This dish is perfect during the fall and winter months because it's so fulfilling on many levels. It's quick and easy, but looks like it took much effort.

❧

In a large skillet over medium-high heat, cook the sausage until lightly browned, about 5 minutes. Drain and return to the skillet.

Add the peas, tomatoes and green chiles, and garlic powder. Reduce the heat to low and simmer 5 minutes. Cover and keep warm.

Lightly grease and preheat a waffle iron. In a large bowl, prepare the cornbread mixes according to the package directions up to the baking instructions. Add the rice, sage, and onion powder.

Spoon 1/2 cup of cornbread mixture into the hot waffle iron. Cook until golden and repeat with the remaining batter. Serve each waffle cut into wedges and topped with the pea stew. Garnish with green onions.

# Black-Eyed Pea Stew with Rice Waffles

**Makes 8 servings**

1 pound Italian sausage (hot or mild), sliced

3 cups cooked black-eyed peas

2 (10-ounce) cans hot diced tomatoes and green chiles

1/2 teaspoon garlic powder

2 (6-ounce) packages cornbread mix

1/2 cup cooked rice

1/2 teaspoon sage

1/2 teaspoon onion powder

Sliced green onions for garnish

# Pull-out-the-Best-China Herbed Squash

**Makes 6 to 8 servings**

2 cups cooked and mashed
yellow squash

3/4 cup grated Swiss cheese

1/2 cup chopped onions

1/4 cup chopped red bell peppers

1/4 cup chopped orange bell peppers

2 eggs, lightly beaten

1/2 cup evaporated milk

4 tablespoons unsalted butter, melted

1 tablespoon sugar

1 tablespoon all-purpose flour

2 tablespoons chopped fresh tarragon

1 tablespoon chopped fresh basil

1/3 cup seasoned dry breadcrumbs

Maybe you're hosting an office lunch or a family birthday. This casserole has something for everyone and makes it an even more festive occasion. It's not your typical squash casserole, thanks to the fresh herbs and colorful bell peppers. Leftovers freeze very well. Just label and use within 3 months for best quality.

Preheat the oven to 350°F. Lightly grease a 2-quart casserole dish and set aside.

In a large bowl, combine the squash, cheese, onions, and peppers. In a separate bowl, whisk together the eggs, milk, butter, sugar, and flour. Add to the vegetables, blending well.

Stir in the tarragon and basil. Pour into the prepared dish and top with the breadcrumbs. Bake 1 hour or until the center is set. Serve warm.

**Note:** Use white or yellow onions for this dish.

## Rogers Farm

Larry Rogers
3831 Northwest 156th Avenue
Gainesville, Florida 32609
(386) 462-2406
Website: www.rogers-farm.com
Consumer Experience: Pick your own, farm stand,
canning classes

Let me place a bet before you that I know I'll win: I double dog dare you to name any variety of peas that I don't like. I love them all and reach for them as a regular comfort food ingredient in Hoppin' John. The way I see it, they are the whole reason things like pepper sauce and chowchow exist.

So it's no wonder that anytime I'm even remotely close to Gainesville, Florida, I make it a point to visit Rogers Farm. Larry Rogers has been making a living farming his whole life, and the 1,000 acres he owns today look like something straight out of a picture book. Row after row of weed-free food is growing as far as you can see. He makes farming look like artwork.

It's the twelve varieties of peas and beans that instantly catch my eye, and I'm immediately dreaming of ways to put them in my tummy. I can see those field peas bubbling away in their own broth on the back burner of the stove. Purple hulls are crowded around chunks of country ham in a large, steaming bowl on my dinner table.

The zipper peas he's famous for are nestled in a mass of country vegetable soup, while pink eyes are being blanched for freezer packaging. The uses to me are endless, so I'm delighted that the rows are equally long.

The farm is open Monday through Saturday, and you'll find the summer season packed with customers. Yet somehow, the staff always make you feel as though you are the only one who matters. The last time I was there, they were hosting a farm birthday party, and it was adorable. It made me wish I were a kid again.

The farm features lots of other summer vegetables. I might make it over to Larry's fresh tomatoes, cucumbers, summer squash, onions, sweet corn, and broad beans, but that's only after my first and largest cooler is packed to the rim with perfect peas.

# Squash Napoleons

Napoleons are usually associated with dessert, but the way these veggies stack, it reminds me of them. And while the presentation is dramatic, it is easy to pull together and serve. Plus, I love food that looks like hands have been all over it!

## Makes 3 servings

1 zucchini, cut on the diagonal into 1/4-inch slices

2 yellow summer squash, cut on the diagonal into 1/4-inch slices

2 garlic cloves, minced

1 teaspoon minced fresh chives

1 teaspoon minced fresh basil

1/8 teaspoon black pepper

2 tablespoons olive oil

olive oil, for drizzling (optional)

fresh cracked black pepper (optional)

Place the zucchini and squash slices in a shallow bowl. Combine the garlic, chives, basil, pepper, and oil and toss over the slices to evenly coat. Marinate at room temperature 30 minutes.

Meanwhile, preheat the oven to 350°F. Spray a baking sheet with nonstick cooking spray. Evenly place the zucchini and squash slices in a single layer on the prepared sheet. Drizzle any leftover marinade over the slices. Roast 40 minutes, turning the slices halfway through.

To serve, place two zucchini slices side by side on a serving plate. Top with 2 slices of the yellow squash, also arranged side by side. Repeat so you have two layers of each; then top with a single slice of the zucchini to connect the two stacks. Drizzle with a little olive oil and add a little fresh cracked black pepper, if desired. Serve immediately.

# Field Pea Fritters

Do you have leftover cooked peas and you don't want to serve them the same way? No problem! I like to use field peas in this concoction, but any variety in this large group of legumes will work.

❧

## Makes 4 servings

Vegetable oil for frying
2 cups cooked field peas
2 eggs, lightly beaten
1 1/2 cups milk
1 cup all-purpose flour
2 teaspoons baking powder
1 teaspoon black pepper
1/2 teaspoon salt
1 tablespoon curry powder
Cocktail sauce

Pour the oil to a depth of 1 inch in a large cast iron skillet and place over medium-high heat. Meanwhile, combine the peas, eggs, and milk in a large mixing bowl. In a separate bowl, combine the flour, baking powder, pepper, salt, and curry. Add to the pea mixture, stirring well to combine.

Carefully drop by tablespoons into the hot grease. Fry 2 minutes, or until lightly browned. Turn over and fry until golden brown. Drain on paper towels and serve warm with cocktail sauce.

# Spring Tonic Spinach

This is a classic side dish that pairs nicely with beef. It has just a bit of heat on the end, thanks to the cayenne. Add more if you want it really hot. The cream cheese softens it and gives it a rich flavor.

❧

## Makes 6 servings

1 tablespoon olive oil
1 sweet onion, peeled and chopped
1 garlic clove, minced
1/2 teaspoon kosher or fine sea salt
1/4 teaspoon black pepper
4 ounces cream cheese
3/4 cup milk
4 cups chopped spinach
1/2 teaspoon cayenne pepper

Place the oil in a large skillet over medium heat. When hot, add the onions and garlic. Cook 7 minutes, stirring frequently. Add the salt, pepper, cream cheese, and milk, stirring constantly until the cheese melts.

Add the spinach to the sauce and cook another 3 to 4 minutes or until it is wilted and soft. Stir in the cayenne just before serving.

Leftover lima beans never had it so good. You'll love how the dressing makes the beans come alive and take on a new life that won't be recognized as last night's leftover side dish. Serve it with any type of fish. I like it with grilled salmon.

# Marinated Lima Beans

**Makes 6 servings**

3 cups cooked lima beans

1 green onion, chopped

2 tablespoons chopped red bell peppers

1/3 cup white wine vinegar

1/4 cup sugar

1/4 cup canola oil

1 tablespoon prepared horseradish

1/4 teaspoon black pepper

Place the beans, onions, and bell peppers in a medium bowl and toss gently to combine. In a jar with a tight-fitting lid, combine the vinegar, sugar, oil, horseradish, and pepper. Shake well to emulsify. Pour over the bean mixture, cover, and refrigerate at least 4 hours and up to 2 days. Toss gently and bring to room temperature before serving.

Parsnips drastically change flavor when they receive a touch of frost from Mother Nature. The starch converts to sugar, and they take on a pleasantly sweet taste. I love the summery flavor these parsnips get from orange juice and pineapple. Serve this dish with grilled fish.

# Setting Sun-Kissed Parsnips

**Makes 4 servings**

1 cup water

1 pound parsnips, peeled and cut into 2-inch strips

1 (8-ounce) can crushed pineapple, undrained

1/2 cup fresh orange juice

2 tablespoons light brown sugar

1/2 teaspoon fresh grated orange zest

Preheat the oven to 350°F. Lightly grease a 1 1/2-quart baking dish and set aside.

Bring the water to a boil in a heavy saucepan over medium-high heat. Add the parsnips. Cover and cook 9 to 10 minutes, or until tender. Drain and transfer to the prepared baking dish.

In a medium bowl, stir together the pineapple and liquid from the can, orange juice, sugar, and orange zest. Blend well. Evenly pour over the parsnips.

Bake 30 minutes, basting occasionally with the liquid. Let stand 5 minutes before serving warm.

Peanut oil adds great flavor and has a high smoke point, so you don't have to worry about the high heat required in this recipe. Peanuts add crunch, giving these beans loads of nutty personality. Serve this quick side dish with just about anything, but it is especially noticeable with ham.

❧

Heat the oil in a large skillet over high heat. Add the beans and sauté, stirring frequently, 5 minutes or until lightly browned.

Reduce the heat to medium and add the stock, peanuts, pepper, and salt. Cook 5 to 7 minutes longer. Remove from the heat and stir in the juice. Serve warm.

# Peanut Sautéed Green Beans

**Makes 6 servings**

1 tablespoon peanut oil

1 1/2 pounds green beans, trimmed and cut in half lengthwise

1/2 cup chicken or vegetable stock

1/4 cup dry roasted peanuts

1/4 teaspoon black pepper

1/8 teaspoon salt

1 tablespoon lemon juice

# Individual Zucchini and Corn Soufflés

**Make this side dish for a dinner party featuring shrimp or roasted pork. It will keep everything on schedule, since the soufflés need to be served right out of the oven. So set your kitchen timer and have everything else ready and the guests seated when the soufflés are done.**

❧

### Makes 4 servings

3 tablespoons unsalted butter, divided

1 1/2 cups shredded zucchini

1/4 cup sliced green onions

3 1/2 tablespoons all-purpose flour

1/2 cup milk

1/4 teaspoon salt

1/8 teaspoon black pepper

3 eggs, separated

1/2 cup creamed corn

2 tablespoons shredded sharp Cheddar cheese

Preheat the oven to 350°F. Lightly grease 4 individual soufflé dishes or 6-ounce custard cups. Place in a 13 x 9-inch baking dish and set aside.

Melt one tablespoon of the butter in a large skillet over medium-high heat. As soon as it begins to foam, add the zucchini and onions. Sauté 4 minutes or until tender. Drain on paper towels and set aside.

Add the remaining butter to the skillet and reduce the heat to low. Stir in the flour and cook 1 minute, whisking constantly to remove the starchy flavor. Gradually add the milk and increase the heat to medium. Cook 3 minutes or until thick and bubbly, whisking constantly. Stir in the salt and pepper.

In a small bowl, whisk the egg yolks until thick. Gradually whisk in a few tablespoons of the hot milk mixture, whisking constantly. Whisk the yolks into the skillet of hot milk and continue to whisk until well combine. Add in the zucchini mixture, corn, and cheese.

In an electric mixer beat the egg whites at high speed until stiff. Fold one-third of the egg whites into the zucchini mixture. Gently fold in the remaining whites.

Using a 2/3 cup measure or ladle, evenly transfer the batter into the prepared soufflé dishes. Add enough hot water to surround the soufflés in the baking dish to a depth of 1 inch.

Bake 22 to 25 minutes or until the soufflés are light brown and puffed. Remove from the water bath and serve immediately.

## Farmers' Market

**Matthews Community
Farmers' Market**

188 North Trade Street
Matthews, North Carolina 28105
(704) 821-6430
Website: www.matthewsfarmersmarket.com
Open year-round
Consumer Experience: Farmers' market

When you link a community with farmers, you strengthen both. That is what the Matthews Community Farmers' Market has been able to accomplish since it humbly began in 1991.

I was first drawn to this beautiful market by the logo, which simply states "Local Folks, Local Farms, Local Food." It was exactly what I was looking for, and evidently, a lot of other customers as well. Historic downtown Matthews is situated in what looks like is right out of a tourist guide book. It's in the Charlotte area, and everything sold there must come from within a 50-mile radius. It has down-home charm written all over it.

Honestly, I'm not sure how local grocery stores compete with this market. You can find eggs, free-range chickens, grass-fed beef, the most incredible mushrooms I've ever eaten, fresh pasta, pastries, cheeses, and remarkable stone-ground grits and cornmeal. Need fresh flowers or plants? It's all there, along with goat's milk lotions, handmade pottery and baskets, and herbal soaps. It's a good thing this place is open year-round!

Oh, and the exceptional produce. Don't forget that. Bring along a wagon for the trip. You'll need it to haul the goodies back to your car, and you'll love every moment of the shopping experience.

# Pocketbook Zucchini

**Zucchini of any shape is stuffed with a salty ham-enhanced breadcrumb filling. It is baked on top of tomatoes, giving you individual servings that are moist and full of flavor. It looks fancy, but it is easy on your pocketbook.**

❧

## Makes 6 servings

4 tablespoons vegetable oil, divided
1 white onion, peeled and coarsely chopped
3 round or long zucchini
2 cups fresh breadcrumbs
1/2 cup chopped fresh parsley
1 cup diced cooked ham
1/2 teaspoon kosher salt
1/4 teaspoon black pepper
2 eggs, lightly beaten
2 tablespoons water
2 garlic cloves, peeled and halved
2 tomatoes, chopped

Preheat the oven to 350°F. Lightly grease a 13 x 9-inch baking dish and set aside.

Place two tablespoons of the oil in a large skillet over medium heat. When hot, add the onions and cook 5 minutes or until softened.

Meanwhile, if using round zucchini, cut off the top quarter and scoop out the insides, leaving a 1/2-inch thick shell. If using long zucchini, trim and cut in half lengthwise. Set aside.

In a mixing bowl, combine the breadcrumbs, parsley, ham, salt, and pepper. Stir in the eggs until well combined. Add the cooked onions, mixing well. Spoon the stuffing into the zucchini. If using round zucchini, cover with the lids, if desired.

Place the water, garlic, and tomatoes in the bottom of the prepared dish. Arrange the zucchini over the tomato mixture in the pan. Drizzle with the remaining oil.

Cover and bake 25 minutes. Uncover and bake 25 minutes longer (remove the round zucchini lids, if using) or until golden brown on the top. To serve, spoon the pan juices and tomato bits over the zucchini.

**Note:** You can prepare this dish ahead by stuffing and refrigerating overnight. Bring to room temperature for 20 minutes before baking as instructed.

Take your pick between hot or mild sausage for this dressing. You could even substitute ground Italian sausage if you want even more flavor. The pecans add a nice crunch, and because it's mixed ahead and refrigerated overnight, this is holiday-worthy dish. It could be served as a brunch item or an anchor for loads of fresh vegetables, like green beans and sliced tomatoes, for dinner.

# Sausage Cornbread Dressing

**Makes 10 servings**

1 pound pork sausage, hot or mild

1 large yellow onion, peeled and chopped

2 large celery ribs, chopped

1 recipe Paprika Cornbread (page 141), cooked, cooled, and crumbled

1 1/2 cups chicken or vegetable stock

1 1/2 cups coarsely chopped pecans

1/4 cup dry sherry

1/4 cup milk

1/4 cup chopped fresh parsley

1/2 teaspoon dried thyme

1/2 teaspoon salt

1/2 teaspoon black pepper

Lightly grease a 13 x 9-inch baking dish and set aside.

In a large skillet over medium heat, cook the sausage until it crumbles and is no longer pink. Remove with a slotted spoon, drain on paper towels, and set aside. Discard all but 1 tablespoon of the pan drippings.

Increase the heat to medium-high. In the same skillet, add the onions and celery to the hot drippings. Sauté 4 minutes or until the onions are just beginning to turn brown.

In a large bowl, combine the sausage, onion mixture, corn-bread, stock, pecans, sherry, milk, parsley, thyme, salt, and pepper. Mix well and transfer to the prepared baking dish. Cover and refrigerate overnight.

Preheat the oven to 350°F. Bring the dressing to room temperature for 30 minutes. Bake 35 to 40 minutes or until heated through. Serve warm.

Throw these gorgeous kabobs on the grill just before you pull off the meat. They cook quickly while the meat rests, so everything will be ready to enjoy at the same time. The peppered oil eliminates any need for salt.

᷍

Soak the skewers in water at least 1 hour before using.

Preheat the grill to medium heat (350°F). Meanwhile, alternate the onions, orange peppers, red peppers, yellow peppers, and green peppers on the skewers. Spray each skewer with cooking spray. Grill 8 to 10 minutes, covered, or until the vegetables are tender, turning frequently.

In a small bowl, combine the vegetable oil, olive oil, garlic, black pepper, red pepper, and white pepper. During the last minute of cooking, brush the oil mixture over the kabobs. Serve warm with any remaining oil mixture drizzled over the top.

# Grilled Mixed Pepper Kabobs

## Makes 8 to 10 servings

10 wooden skewers

1 large purple onion, peeled and cut into wedges

1 large orange bell pepper, seeded and cut into wedges

1 large red bell pepper, seeded and cut into wedges

1 large yellow bell pepper, seeded and cut into wedges

1 large green bell pepper, seeded and cut into wedges

Nonstick cooking spray

2 tablespoons vegetable oil

1 tablespoon olive oil

1 garlic clove, minced

$1/4$ teaspoon black pepper

$1/4$ teaspoon red pepper

$1/4$ teaspoon white pepper

# Parsnip and Tart Apple Puree

The elegance of this dish is unbelievable, and even if you think you don't like parsnips, give it a try. I love it dearly with roasted pork. They are especially plentiful during the fall and winter months. Select parsnips as you would potatoes. Refrigerate in a plastic bag in the crisper drawer for up to 2 weeks.

∼

**Makes 4 servings**

3 cups water

1 1/2 pounds parsnips, peeled and chopped

2 tablespoons unsalted butter

1 yellow onion, peeled and chopped

2 Granny Smith apples, peeled, cored, and chopped

1/4 cup sour cream

1/2 teaspoon kosher salt

1/4 teaspoon black pepper

1/8 teaspoon allspice

Place the water in a heavy saucepan over medium-high heat and bring to a boil. Add the parsnips, cover, and cook 15 to 20 minutes or until very tender.

Meanwhile, place the butter in a large skillet over medium heat. As it begins to foam, add the onions and apples. Cook 7 to 9 minutes, stirring constantly until the apples are tender.

Drain the parsnips, reserving 1/4 cup of the cooking liquid. Transfer the parsnips to a food processor and add the apple mixture. Puree until smooth. Add the sour cream, salt, pepper, and allspice. Puree until smooth.

Add 1 tablespoon of the reserved cooking liquid at a time until the desired consistency is reached. Transfer to a bowl and serve warm.

## The Curb Market

221 North Church Street
Hendersonville, North Carolina 28792
(828) 692-8012
Website: www.curbmarket.com
Opens at 8:00 a.m. every Tuesday, Thursday,
and Saturday
Consumer Experience: Farmers' market

The Curb Market in Hendersonville, North Carolina, is the oldest farm market in the South. Established in 1924, it began as a way for agricultural producers throughout the county to sell their items to "city folk." The market soon became a vital farm link for those who ran boardinghouses and has morphed into the same kind of connection today for folks who want to know who grew their food.

At 8:00 a.m. every Tuesday, Thursday, and Saturday, you have a homegrown supermarket in front of you. It's full of every imaginable locally grown produce item, as well as jams, jellies, pickles, relishes, canned goods, plants, herbs, and flowers. But I have to make a beeline straight to Donald and Donna Thompson, who make the best homemade cinnamon rolls I've ever put in my mouth.

I make it a point to visit on the last Saturday in September for the Curb Market's twice-yearly "Ol' Timey Days." Early that morning, a huge breakfast of biscuits, country ham, sausage, and gravy has been prepared on wood-burning stoves and is ready for everyone.

While my husband spends the morning visiting the old farm equipment and cars, I'm busy in the areas housing produce and handmade crafts. I am a fan of the handcrafted birdhouses, quilts, and rugs that decorate the stalls there in North Carolina and soon, my home and yard in Tennessee.

Trust me, you will find plenty of reasons to make this recipe after one taste. The blue cheese makes it an excellent selection to serve with beef. Choose cabbage heads that are compact and tight. Keep cabbage refrigerated for up to a week before shredding to make this delicious, tangy slaw.

# Blue Cheese and Bacon Coleslaw

In a large bowl, toss together the cabbage, cheese, and bacon. In a separate small bowl, whisk together the mayonnaise, vinegar, honey, salt, and pepper. Gently toss over the coleslaw mixture. Cover and refrigerate at least 30 minutes before serving.

## Makes 10 servings

1 head cabbage, shredded

1 cup crumbled blue cheese

8 bacon slices, cooked and crumbled

3/4 cup mayonnaise

2 tablespoons red wine vinegar

1 tablespoon honey

1/4 teaspoon salt

1/8 teaspoon black pepper

# Breads

Basil Biscuits

Blue Cheese Biscuits

Cheddar Muffin Pan Biscuits

Grapefruit Biscuits

Hot Cheddar Cornbread

Revival Strawberry Bread

Cornmeal Yeast Muffins

Hot Water Ham Cornbread

Fresh Chive Spoon Bread

Heat Lovers' Spoon Bread

Paprika Cornbread

Pack a Picnic Pepper Muffins

Sage Cornbread Muffins

Speckled Cornbread

Sweet Corn Muffins

Dried Pear Bacon Bread

Hot Water Cornbread

These savory biscuits are great for holding slices of roasted pork or beef. Always cut biscuits with a cutter rather than an upside-down drinking glass that has no cutting edge. One that measures 2 inches in diameter is the standard.

❧

In a medium bowl, combine the yeast and water. Let stand 5 minutes. Stir in the buttermilk and set aside.

In a mixing bowl, stir together the flour, sugar, baking powder, baking soda, and salt. With a pastry blender or two forks, cut in the shortening until the mixture crumbles. Add the buttermilk mixture, basil, and tomatoes, stirring just until moistened. The dough will be sticky.

Transfer the dough to a heavily floured surface and knead 5 times. Roll to 1/2-inch thickness and cut with a 2-inch cutter. Place on a lightly greased cast iron biscuit baker or baking sheet. Cover and let rise 30 minutes in a warm place free from drafts.

Meanwhile, preheat the oven to 450°F. Bake 10 to 12 minutes or until golden brown. Serve warm.

# Basil Biscuits

Makes 12 biscuits

1 (1/4-ounce) package active dry yeast
2 tablespoons hot water (110°F to 115°F)
1 cup buttermilk
2 1/2 cups all-purpose flour
2 tablespoons sugar
1 1/2 teaspoons baking powder
1/2 teaspoon baking soda
1/4 teaspoon salt
1/2 cup vegetable shortening or lard
1/4 cup chopped fresh basil
2 tablespoons finely chopped oil-packed sun-dried tomatoes, drained

# Blue Cheese Biscuits

There is hardly a better complement for a slice of country ham than these tangy cheese biscuits. Invest in a good, sturdy rolling pin if you don't already have one. It makes biscuitmaking quick and easy.

◌

## Makes 7 servings

1 (3-ounce) package blue cheese, crumbled

2 tablespoons finely chopped fresh chives

1 teaspoon dried basil

$1/2$ teaspoon dried thyme

2 cups all-purpose flour

1 tablespoon baking powder

$1/2$ teaspoon salt

$1/4$ teaspoon baking soda

6 tablespoons unsalted butter, cut into pieces

$3/4$ cup buttermilk

Preheat the oven to 450°F. Lightly grease a cast iron biscuit baker or baking sheet and set aside. In a small bowl, combine the cheese, chives, basil, and thyme. Set aside.

In a large bowl, combine the flour, baking powder, salt, and baking soda. Cut in the cheese mixture and butter with a pastry blender or two forks until the mixture resembles coarse meal. Make a well in the center and stir in the buttermilk.

Transfer the dough to a lightly floured surface and knead 7 times. Roll the dough to $1/2$-inch thickness and cut with a 2-inch cutter. Transfer to the prepared pan and bake 13 to 15 minutes or until golden brown. Serve warm.

Normally, biscuits are not muffin shaped, but these are great for serving with salads and homemade stews. Use lard if you have it for the flakiest, most tender biscuits. It is richer than other fats and will give you the best results.

Preheat the oven to 400°F. Lightly grease a 12-cup muffin pan and set aside.

Place the flour, baking powder, and salt in a mixing bowl. Cut in the lard with a pastry blender or two forks until the mixture resembles coarse meal. Add the milk and cheese.

Transfer to a lightly floured surface and knead gently and quickly, no more than 5 times. Drop evenly by tablespoons into the prepared pan. Sprinkle the tops evenly with the paprika. Bake 12 to 15 minutes or until golden brown. Serve hot.

# Cheddar Muffin Pan Biscuits

**Makes 10 to 12 biscuits**

2 cups all-purpose flour

3 teaspoons baking powder

1 teaspoon salt

4 tablespoons lard or vegetable shortening

1 cup milk

3/4 cup Cheddar cheese, shredded

1 teaspoon paprika

Split these zippy biscuits and fill with small slices of country ham. You'll love the citrus flavor of the biscuits next to the salty meat. A cast iron biscuit baker is round with a handle and perfectly holds a recipe of biscuits. The even heating of cast iron makes it the best baking pan for bread.

Preheat the oven to 425°F. Lightly grease a cast iron biscuit baker or baking sheet and set aside.

In a mixing bowl, combine the flour, sugar, baking soda, and salt. Using a pastry blender or two forks, cut in the lard until the mixture resembles coarse meal. Stir in the juice just until the mixture is moistened.

Transfer the dough to a lightly floured surface and knead 5 times. Roll to 1/2-inch thickness and cut with a 2-inch cutter. Place on the prepared pan. Bake 10 minutes or until golden brown. Serve warm.

# Grapefruit Biscuits

**Makes 12 biscuits**

2 cups all-purpose flour

1 tablespoon sugar

1 teaspoon baking soda

1/2 teaspoon salt

1/4 cup lard or vegetable shortening

1/2 cup plus 1 tablespoon grapefruit juice

## Kenny's Farmhouse Cheese

Kenny Mattingly
2033 Thomerson Park Road
Austin, Kentucky 42123
(888) 571-4029
E-mail: Kenny@kennyscheese.com
Website: www.kennysfarmhousecheese.com
Consumer Experience: Tour, general store, purchase
online, purchase in retail outlets

When most of us say we are going to take a trip to visit farms, we usually carry a picnic basket and head out to the local countryside. When Kenny Mattingly wanted to do the same thing back in the 1990s, he headed to western Europe.

When Kenny returned home to Kentucky, his trip resulted in a total revamping of his family dairy business into a farmhouse cheese operation. His philosophy is that if you are going to dream, dream big! Fast-forward to the present and Kenny Mattingly has not only saved his 200-acre family dairy farm, but he's become an award-winning cheesemaker with a reputation for having the best cheese you can find.

More than 70,000 pounds of fresh milk cheese were produced last year, and Kenny's Farmhouse Cheese is still moving full speed ahead. The most difficult part for the customer is narrowing down the selection of what to purchase. I know because that's my problem every time I visit. You think you've found your favorite—until you taste the next variety.

There are numerous versions of Asiago, Colby, Cheddar, Gouda, Gruyère, Havarti, Monterey Jack, Swiss, and truly outstanding blue cheese varieties. Each has its own special characteristics and is sold in half-pound blocks. The depth of flavor will astound you, and you'll never purchase mass-produced supermarket cheese again. I'm so glad Kenny took a leap of faith and followed his dream. For all of us, he has certainly made the cheese world a better place indeed.

What kind of Southerner doesn't throw cheese into nearly everything she makes? None that I know! These cut wedges are great when you have grilled fish, chicken, or turkey planned for dinner.

≈

Preheat the oven to 400°F. Place a greased 10-inch cast iron skillet in the oven to heat while the desired temperature is reached.

Meanwhile, in a large bowl, mix together the cornmeal, flour, sugar, baking powder, salt, and baking soda, stirring gently. Make a well in the center and add the buttermilk, butter, and eggs. Stir in the corn, cheese, and peppers, if desired.

Pour the batter into the preheated skillet. Bake 35 to 40 minutes. Immediately transfer to a serving dish. Cool 3 minutes before cutting into wedges.

# Hot Cheddar Cornbread

**Makes 8 to 10 servings**

1 3/4 cups plain cornmeal

1 3/4 cups all-purpose flour

1/4 cup sugar

1 tablespoon baking powder

1 1/2 teaspoons salt

1/2 teaspoon baking soda

1 1/2 cups buttermilk

7 tablespoons unsalted butter, melted

3 eggs, lightly beaten

1 cup fresh sweet corn kernels

1 1/2 cups grated sharp Cheddar cheese

2 tablespoons chopped jalapeños, optional

# Revival Strawberry Bread

**This quick bread will change the way you enjoy breakfast. It gets a bit of crunch from almonds, or you can substitute pecans or walnuts. Toasted slices need nothing more than a slather of softened butter.**

❧

### Makes 2 loaves

3 cups all-purpose flour

2 cups sugar

1 tablespoon ground cinnamon

1 teaspoon baking soda

1 teaspoon salt

4 eggs, lightly beaten

1¼ cups vegetable oil

2 cups diced strawberries

1 cup chopped almonds

Preheat the oven to 350°F. Lightly grease two loaf pans and set aside.

In a large mixing bowl, combine the flour, sugar, cinnamon, baking soda, and salt. Add the eggs and oil, stirring just until moistened. Fold in the strawberries and almonds.

Divide the batter evenly between the two loaf pans. Bake 1 hour or until a tester inserted in the center comes out clean. Cool in the pans 5 minutes. Remove and cool completely on wire racks before slicing and serving.

**Note:** These loaves freeze beautifully. Use within 3 months for best quality.

# Cornmeal Yeast Muffins

### Makes 3 dozen muffins

1 (1/4-ounce) package active dry yeast

1/4 cup hot water (110°F to 115°F)

1 3/4 cups milk

1/3 cup sugar

1/4 cup vegetable oil

4 tablespoons unsalted butter

1 teaspoon salt

2 eggs

1 1/2 cups plain cornmeal

5 1/4 cups all-purpose flour, divided

**These are not ordinary yeast muffins, thanks to the addition of crunchy cornmeal. They are a cross between light, airy yeast bread and corn-bread. An added bonus is that the leftovers freeze well. Serve with soups, stews, or slices of baked ham.**

In a mixing bowl, dissolve the yeast in the water and let stand undisturbed for 5 minutes.

Meanwhile, in a medium saucepan over low heat, combine the milk, sugar, oil, butter, and salt. Cook, stirring constantly, until the butter melts and the mixture is well blended. Set aside to cool to 105°F.

Add the milk mixture to the yeast, stirring well. Add the eggs, cornmeal, and 2 cups of the flour. Beat with an electric mixer at medium speed until smooth. Add the remaining flour, blending well.

Turn the dough onto a lightly floured surface and knead 8 minutes or until smooth and elastic. Place in a greased bowl, turning to evenly grease the dough. Cover and let rise in a warm place free from drafts 1 hour or until doubled in size.

Lightly grease 36 muffin cups and set aside. Punch the dough down and shape it into 72 balls. Place 2 balls in each cup. Let rise 45 minutes or until doubled in size.

Preheat the oven to 375°F. Bake 12 to 15 minutes or until golden brown. Remove from the pans immediately. Serve warm or cool to room temperature.

## McEwen and Sons

Frank McEwen
30620 Highway 25 South
P.O. Box 439
Wilsonville, Alabama 35186
(205) 669-6605
Website: www.coosavalleymilling.com
Consumer Experience: General store, local delivery,
purchase in local retail outlets

Wow! That was my first reaction to the marvelous stone-ground grits I purchased from McEwen and Sons in a little community known as Wilsonville, Alabama. Flavor was over-the-top, and the grits even smelled fresh. I was an instant fan, and you will be too.

Frank McEwen has been operating the Coosa Valley Milling Company for more than 30 years, where it has been the go-to feed and supply store for local farmers. The addition of a burrstone gristmill is what got my attention. In addition to their certified organic grits, you can purchase yellow, white, and blue cornmeal, as well as polenta.

Don't worry about the season when stopping by the store. They are open year-round Monday through Saturday. Frank's father heads a delightful side business guiding his grandsons in raising chickens in an antibiotic- and hormone-free environment. Their meat is also sold at the family store. The fresh eggs are gathered daily from cage-free hens, and the taste is remarkable. Who knew a milling company could be a must-stop place?

# Hot Water Ham Cornbread

**Half-and-half enriches this batter, and bits of leftover country ham elevate this bread to a meal in itself for those on the go. As with any hot water bread, prepare this at the last possible minute so it will be hot when served.**

⌘

**Makes 8 servings**

Canola oil

2 cups plain cornmeal

1 1/4 teaspoons salt

1 teaspoon sugar

1/4 teaspoon baking powder

1/4 cup half-and-half

1 tablespoon vegetable oil

3/4 cup boiling water

1 cup finely chopped country ham

Pour the canola oil to a depth of 1/2 inch in a large cast iron skillet. Place over medium-high heat.

Meanwhile, in a mixing bowl, combine the cornmeal, salt, sugar, and baking powder. Make a well in the center and stir in the half-and-half and vegetable oil. Gradually add the boiling water, stirring until the batter is the consistency of cooked grits. Fold in the ham.

With a 1/4-cup measure, drop the batter into the hot oil. Fry 3 minutes on each side or until golden brown. Drain on paper towels. Repeat with the remaining batter. Serve hot.

**Calhoun's Country Hams**

Tom Calhoun
219 South East Street
Culpeper, Virginia 22701
(540) 825-8319 or 1-877-825-8319
Website: www.calhounhams.com
Consumer Experience: Purchase online, at local
farmers market, and in retail outlets

Country ham making is an art, and those who do it well are as talented as any traditional artist I know. It demands patience, knowledge, perfect timing, and age-old traditions that cannot be learned from a book.

Tom Calhoun is one such master artist. Like most who practice the same craft, Tom learned this art form through working with his grandfather.

Known in Virginia as the "Ham Man," Tom has perfected his preservation technique so you aren't overwhelmed with the taste of salt at first bite. It is a welcome refinement, and the meat takes on an almost silky texture due to the increase in moisture. I'm hooked!

I purchase the ham uncooked, but cooked ham is also available, as well as country sausage. The best deals are the whole ham and the half ham, both remarkable. Smaller portions of center-cut slices, side meat, and ends and pieces that are great for throwing into the bean pot are just as tasty and are priced by the pound. If you aren't going to be in the area, purchase Tom's delicious hams online.

Country hams are such an integral part of our Southern heritage . . . finely laced through the years with our progression of passing farm food to those who have no connection to the farm. Make sure you purchase it from the best, like Tom Calhoun in Culpeper, Virginia.

Spoon bread is so named because it takes a spoon or fork to eat it. And when your fresh chives need a haircut, this is the recipe to pull out and make. It will seem like a lot of chives, but their already mild flavor will mellow even more in the oven.

༄

Preheat the oven to 350°F. Lightly grease a 1 1/2-quart baking dish and set aside.

In a heavy saucepan over medium-high heat, stir together the milk, water, butter, salt, and pepper. Bring to a simmer and gradually whisk in the cornmeal. Reduce the heat to medium-low and whisk constantly 3 minutes or until the mixture begins to pull away from the sides of the pan. Remove from the heat and stir in the sour cream.

In a medium bowl, beat the eggs until thick, around 2 minutes. Gradually add 1 cup of the cornmeal mixture, whisking constantly. Stir the egg mixture back into the cornmeal mixture. Add the cheese and chives, stirring constantly until the cheese melts.

Transfer to the prepared baking dish. Bake 35 to 40 minutes or until a tester inserted in the center comes out clean. Let stand five minutes before serving warm.

# Fresh Chive Spoon Bread

**Makes 6 to 8 servings**

2 cups milk

1/2 cup water

2 tablespoons unsalted butter

1 teaspoon salt

1/2 teaspoon black pepper

1 cup self-rising cornmeal

2/3 cup sour cream

4 eggs

1 1/2 cups shredded Cheddar cheese

1/2 cup chopped fresh chives

# Heat Lovers' Spoon Bread

**I adore hot peppers and frequently double the amount called for in this recipe. You can start out slow and see how much your family wants to have it notched up! This is terrific served with roasted turkey or chicken.**

❧

Preheat the oven to 350°F. Grease a 1 1/2-quart baking dish and set aside.

In the bowl of an electric mixer, beat the egg whites until stiff peaks form. Set aside.

In a mixing bowl, whisk together the cornmeal and 1 cup of the milk. Set aside.

Place the remaining milk in a heavy saucepan over medium-high heat. Bring to a simmer and reduce the heat to medium-low. Whisk in the cornmeal mixture and stir constantly until thick and bubbly, around 9 minutes.

Remove from the heat and stir in the butter, salt, and sugar. Blend well. Add the egg yolks, one at a time, mixing well after each addition. Stir in the onions and jalapeños. Gently fold in the egg whites.

Transfer to the prepared pan and bake 55 minutes to 1 hour or until a tester inserted in the center comes out clean. Let stand 5 minutes and serve warm.

## Makes 6 servings

4 eggs, separated
1 cup self-rising cornmeal
3 cups milk, divided
2 tablespoons unsalted butter, softened
1 teaspoon salt
1/8 teaspoon sugar
1/2 cup chopped onions
1 to 2 jalapeños, seeded and minced

Paprika is ground, dried, aromatic sweet red pepper pods. The color of this cornbread is gorgeous thanks to this seasoning that is all too often used just as a garnish. Serve this with wild game or grass-fed beef.

# Paprika Cornbread

∽

Preheat the oven to 450°F. Place a greased 9-inch cast iron skillet in the oven to heat while the desired oven temperature is reached.

In a mixing bowl, combine the cornmeal, biscuit mix, sugar, paprika, baking powder, salt, baking soda, and pepper, blending well. Make a well in the center and add the eggs, buttermilk, and drippings. Stir until moistened.

Pour into the preheated skillet. Bake 25 to 30 minutes or until golden brown. Immediately transfer to a serving plate and cool 3 minutes. Cut into wedges and serve hot.

## Makes 8 servings

1 1/2 cups plain cornmeal

2/3 cup biscuit mix

1 tablespoon plus 1 teaspoon sugar

1 1/2 teaspoons paprika

1 1/2 teaspoons baking powder

1 teaspoon salt

1/2 teaspoon baking soda

1/4 teaspoon white pepper

2 eggs, lightly beaten

1 1/2 cups buttermilk

2 tablespoons bacon drippings, melted

# Pack a Picnic Pepper Muffins

### Makes 16 muffins

2 1/2 cups all-purpose flour

2 tablespoons baking powder

1/2 teaspoon salt

3/4 cup shredded Gruyère or sharp Cheddar cheese

1 (2-ounce) jar diced pimiento peppers, drained

1/4 cup self-rising cornmeal

1/4 cup sugar

1/4 cup finely chopped onions

3 tablespoons finely chopped green bell peppers

1/4 teaspoon cayenne pepper

2 eggs, beaten

1 1/2 cups milk

1/4 cup vegetable oil

Pimientos and sweet bells make these muffins a must to take along on a nontraditional picnic. Serve with sliced fruit and cheese. Or you can serve them with hot soup or on a brunch buffet. Any leftovers can easily be frozen. Use within 2 months for best quality.

❧

Preheat the oven to 400°F. Lightly grease 16 muffin cups and set aside.

Combine the flour, baking powder, salt, cheese, and pimientos in a large mixing bowl. Add the cornmeal, sugar, onions, bell peppers, and cayenne, mixing until combined.

Make a well in the center. In a separate bowl, combine the eggs, milk, and oil. Add to the dry ingredients, stirring just until the mixture is combined. Spoon evenly into the prepared muffin cups, filling two-thirds full. Bake 20 to 25 minutes. Transfer immediately to wire racks and cool or serve warm.

**Note:** For mini muffins, cut the baking time in half.

# Sage Cornbread Muffins

Every year, I dry sage from my herb garden. I package the dried whole leaves in canning jars and resist the urge to crumble them until I am ready to add sage to recipes. It has such a nice, strong flavor and transforms these muffins into a great brunch bread. Serve them with sausage to accentuate the sage flavor in both.

**Makes 12 servings**

1 1/2 cups self-rising cornmeal mix
1 1/2 teaspoons dried sage
1/2 teaspoon poultry seasoning
1 1/2 cups buttermilk
4 tablespoons unsalted butter, melted
1 egg, beaten

Preheat the oven to 450°F. Generously grease a 12-cup cast iron muffin pan and place in the oven to heat while the desired oven temperature is reached.

Meanwhile, in a medium bowl, combine the cornmeal, sage, and poultry seasoning. Make a well in the center and add the buttermilk, butter, and egg, mixing well.

Evenly spoon the batter into the preheated cups. Bake 20 minutes or until golden brown. Immediately remove from the muffin pan and serve hot.

# Speckled Cornbread

## Makes 8 servings

1 cup plain cornmeal

3/4 cup all-purpose flour

2 tablespoons chopped green onions, green parts only

1 tablespoon sugar

2 teaspoons baking powder

1/2 teaspoon baking soda

1/2 teaspoon salt

1/2 teaspoon chili powder

1/4 teaspoon ground cumin

1 cup plain yogurt

1 egg

2 tablespoons vegetable oil

1 (2-ounce) jar diced pimientos, drained

The small amount of sugar used in this cornbread brings out the nutty flavor of the cornmeal. The yogurt keeps the bread from becoming dry. Purchase local stone-ground cornmeal, and store it in your refrigerator or freezer until ready to use. This bread is really nice with a fresh vegetable dinner or simple soup.

Preheat the oven to 400°F. Place an 8-inch greased cast iron skillet in the oven while the desired temperature is reached.

Meanwhile, in a mixing bowl, combine the cornmeal, flour, onions, sugar, baking powder, baking soda, salt, chili powder, and cumin. Make a well in the center and set aside.

In a small mixing bowl, stir together the yogurt, egg, oil, and pimientos. Add to the cornmeal mixture and stir just until moistened.

Pour into the prepared skillet and bake 22 to 25 minutes or until golden brown. Immediately transfer to a serving plate. Cut into wedges and serve hot.

These muffins are what Southerners call "ever so slightly sweet," thanks to the maple syrup and honey. Serve them with baked ham or slices of grilled turkey tenderloin.

# Sweet Corn Muffins

**Makes 12 muffins**

1 1/2 cups all-purpose flour
1 cup plain cornmeal
1/2 cup sugar
1 tablespoon baking powder
3/4 teaspoon salt
1/2 cup (1 stick) unsalted butter, melted
3/4 cup milk
2 eggs
2 tablespoons maple syrup or sorghum syrup
2 tablespoons honey

Preheat the oven to 375°F. Grease a 12-cup muffin pan and set aside.

In a large bowl, mix together the flour, cornmeal, sugar, baking powder, and salt. Stir in the butter until well blended.

In a small bowl, whisk together the milk, eggs, syrup, and honey. Add to the flour mixture, stirring until just combined (the batter will be slightly lumpy). Spoon evenly into the prepared muffin cups.

Bake 20 to 22 minutes or until a tester inserted in the center of the muffin comes out clean. Cool in the pan on a wire rack 10 minutes. Loosen the muffins with the tip of a knife and remove. Serve warm or cool completely on a wire rack.

**Note:** These muffins freeze very well. Label and use within 2 months for best quality.

# Dried Pear Bacon Bread

### Makes 1 loaf

1/2 cup finely chopped dried pears

1/4 cup dry white wine

5 bacon slices, chopped

1 1/2 cups shredded sharp Cheddar cheese

1/3 cup chopped walnuts, toasted

1 tablespoon minced fresh sage

1 3/4 cups all-purpose flour

1 tablespoon baking powder

1/2 teaspoon salt

1/4 teaspoon black pepper

3 eggs

1/2 cup milk

1/3 cup vegetable oil

**This quick bread is actually better the day after it is made, so plan ahead and you'll be rewarded appropriately! My neighbor gives me pears every year, and I dry them in my food processor. If you aren't so lucky to have trees nearby, go to a local producer in the fall. The dried pears are rehydrated in wine, giving this bread great depth of flavor.**

Preheat the oven to 350°F and position the rack in the center of the oven. Lightly grease and flour a loaf pan and set aside.

Combine the pears and wine and set aside to soften.

In a large skillet over medium heat, cook the bacon until crisp, around 7 minutes. Drain on paper towels.

In a mixing bowl, combine the bacon, cheese, walnuts, and sage. In a separate bowl, whisk together the flour, baking powder, salt, and pepper. Add to the cheese mixture.

In the previously used flour bowl, whisk together the eggs, milk, and oil. Drain the pears from the wine and add to the cheese mixture, along with the egg mixture. Stir just until the dry ingredients are incorporated.

Transfer the dough (it will be sticky) to the prepared pan. Bake about 55 minutes or until golden brown on top and a tester inserted in the center comes out clean. Cool in the pan 5 minutes before removing and cooling completely on a wire rack.

There is nothing in the world that goes better with tomato soup than this . . . not even grilled cheese sandwiches! These hot cakes should always be served that way, so have the rest of the meal practically on the table when these hit the skillet.

༄

Bring the water to a boil in a saucepan over medium-high heat.

Meanwhile, combine the cornmeal, salt, and baking powder in a mixing bowl. Pour oil 1 inch deep into a large cast iron skillet and place over medium heat.

Add 1/2 cup of the boiling water to the cornmeal mixture, mixing thoroughly. Add more water as needed to maintain a thick consistency (similar to really thick cooked grits). Take tablespoons of the batter and flatten in the palm of your hand.

With a slotted spatula, lower into the hot oil. Fry 4 minutes or until golden brown. Drain on paper towels. Serve hot.

# Hot Water Cornbread

**Makes 6 servings**

4 cups water
2 cups plain cornmeal
3/4 teaspoon salt
1/2 teaspoon baking powder
Vegetable oil or melted shortening for frying

# Entrees

Show-Off Grilled Cheese Sandwiches

Southern Cornbread Supreme

Baked Parmesan Catfish

Nut-Crusted Catfish

Southern Catfish Cakes

Shrimp-Stuffed Catfish Rolls

Open-Faced Cajun Shrimp Sandwiches

Bayou Crawfish Casserole

Rosemary Shrimp

Spiced Pork Pot Pie

Grilled Pork Loin with Fresh Tomato
    Marmalade

Spinach-Stuffed Pork Roll

Sassy Pecan and Beet Sandwiches

Chicken Croquettes with Cherry Tomato
    Puree

Quick Sautéed Chicken Livers with Fresh
    Corn Sauce

Confetti Chicken Salad

Roasted Chicken Pecan Salad

Skillet Thighs

What a Catch! Fish Cakes

Well-Dressed Flounder Rolls

Meal-on-a-Stick Lamb Kabobs

Special-Occasion Stuffed Eggplant

Spiced Lentil Chili

Divine from the Vine Tomato Sauce

Easy Crust Chicken Pot Pie

Winter Solace Chicken and Dumplings

Traditional Southern Pot Roast

Skillet-Fried Chicken

Every now and then, you need to make something different! These semisoft cheeses melt like a dream to form a substantial and sensational sandwich. Use thick slices of really nice bread to hold the melted cheese elegantly.

❧

In a small bowl, combine the butter, thyme, Parmesan, and garlic. Spread evenly on one side of each bread slice.

Lightly grease a griddle or a large skillet and place over medium heat. Carefully sprinkle a couple drops of water on the griddle. When they sizzle and jump around, the griddle is ready. Place four slices of bread, butter side down, on the hot griddle. Layer the sandwiches with a slice of each cheese and a tomato slice, if desired. Brown 3 to 4 minutes on each side. Cut in half and serve warm.

# Show-Off Grilled Cheese Sandwiches

**Makes 4 sandwiches**

4 tablespoons unsalted butter, softened

1 tablespoon chopped fresh thyme

1 tablespoon grated Parmesan or Romano cheese

1 garlic clove, minced

8 slices 3/4-inch thick sandwich bread

4 slices Gouda or Havarti cheese

4 slices fontina cheese

4 slices mozzarella or provolone cheese

1 sliced Roma tomato, optional

# Southern Cornbread Supreme

This casserole is a complete meal and can be made all winter long, after the garden is lost until spring. I pull bits and pieces of cooked peas and corn that always seem to hide in my freezer to stir into the mix. This dish is warm, hearty, filling, inexpensive, and smells like something your grandmother would have made.

❧

## Makes 8 servings

1 pound ground beef

1 medium white onion, peeled and chopped

1 cup plain cornmeal

1/2 cup all-purpose flour

1/2 teaspoon baking soda

2 eggs, lightly beaten

1 cup buttermilk

1/4 cup vegetable oil

1 cup cooked black-eyed peas

1 cup creamed sweet corn

1 cup shredded Cheddar cheese

1 teaspoon salt

1 teaspoon black pepper

2 pickled jalapen?os, chopped

Preheat the oven to 325°F. Lightly grease an 11 x 7-inch baking dish and set aside.

In a large skillet over medium heat, brown the beef, stirring until it crumbles and no pink remains. With a slotted spoon, remove the ground beef from the pan and set aside to drain on paper towels. Add the onions and brown 5 minutes in the pan drippings. Drain and set aside.

In a large mixing bowl, combine the cornmeal, flour, and baking soda. Make a well in the center and add the eggs, buttermilk, and oil, stirring just until moistened. Add the reserved beef and onions. Stir in the peas, corn, cheese, salt, pepper, and jalapen?os, mixing well.

Spread into the prepared pan and bake 1 hour. Serve hot.

Salty Parmesan cheese not only adds flavor but also provides the crispy crust for this low-fat recipe. Catfish is a truly Southern specialty, with a firm flesh and a mild taste. The name comes from the barbells that hang down around the mouth of the fish, resembling cat whiskers.

∽

Preheat the oven to 350°F. Lightly grease a 13 x 9-inch baking pan and set aside.

In a shallow bowl, combine the Parmesan, flour, paprika, salt, and pepper. In separate bowl, beat the egg and milk.

Dip the fillets into the egg mixture and dredge in the Parmesan mixture. Arrange in the prepared baking dish. Bake uncovered 20 minutes or until the fish flakes easily with a fork. Serve immediately.

# Baked Parmesan Catfish

**Makes 4 servings**

1/3 cup shredded Parmesan cheese
2 tablespoons all-purpose flour
1/2 teaspoon paprika
1/4 teaspoon garlic or seasoned salt
1/8 teaspoon black pepper
1 egg
2 tablespoons milk
4 catfish fillets (about 4 ounces each)

Not every catfish fillet has to be fried to be crispy. The crunchy coating from this recipe is made possible by crushed crackers and slivered almonds. A thin smear of mayonnaise holds it onto the fillets while it happily bakes in the oven. You can substitute flounder or orange roughy for the catfish if desired.

∽

Preheat the oven to 400°F. Place the oil and lemon juice in a 13 x 9-inch baking dish, tilting it to evenly spread. Arrange the fillets in a single layer on top of the juice mixture. Sprinkle evenly with the salt and pepper. Spread the mayonnaise evenly over the fillets and set aside.

In a small bowl, combine the crumbs, butter, and almonds, mixing well. Sprinkle over the fillets. Bake 12 to 14 minutes, or until the fish flakes easily with a fork. Serve hot.

# Nut–Crusted Catfish

**Makes 4 servings**

1 tablespoon olive oil
2 teaspoons lemon juice
1 pound catfish fillets
1/4 teaspoon salt
1/4 teaspoon black pepper
3 tablespoons mayonnaise
1/2 cup butter cracker crumbs
3 tablespoons unsalted butter, melted
1/4 cup slivered almonds, toasted

## Delta Pride Catfish

1301 Industrial Parkway
Indianola, Mississippi 38751
(800) 228-3474
E-mail: pwalker@deltapride.com
Website: www.deltapride.com
Consumer Experience: Tour, purchase online,
purchase in retail outlets

The Mississippi Delta is a region unlike any other in the U.S. The land is extremely flat and full of rich nutrients. It's also catfish country, and you'll see the distinct ponds practically everywhere you look.

Delta Pride is a 160-farmer member co-op that has been in business nearly 20 years. Based 25 miles east of the mighty Mississippi River, in Indianola, Mississippi, it is the largest farm-raised catfish processor in the world. The co-op controls more than 65,000 acres of catfish ponds throughout Mississippi and Arkansas.

Even though the industry began in the 1960s, it wasn't until the 1980s that 116

farmers came together to form the co-op. The reason? They were having trouble selling their products individually. As a group, they had more bargaining power, and soon, the industry made a turn and embraced the freshwater product.

Today, 75 percent of all the catfish consumed in the U.S. comes from the Mississippi Delta region. The average pond covers around 12 acres and is close to 4 feet deep. The fish are harvested every week of the year. And while you can't catch your own catfish at Delta Pride, it is a fascinating journey to learn how the industry started and has progressed to turn this flatland to gold.

All of the members' ponds are located within 50 miles of the three primary plants. The main plant is at the co-op headquarters in Indianola. The second plant is in Belzoni, the county with the most water acres in catfish production in Mississippi. The third is 4 miles south of Indianola, near Inverness. The area has been dubbed "the Catfish Capitol of the World," and a drive there is all it takes to see why.

This dish is the Southern version of crab cakes and can serve as a entrée or an appetizer. Either way, it's evenly golden and crispy on the outside while slightly spicy and light on the inside. I usually serve them on a bed of salad greens.

❧

Preheat the oven to 350°F. Lightly grease a baking sheet and add the fillets in a single layer. Sprinkle evenly with the salt. Bake 10 minutes or until the fish flakes easily with a fork. Cool on a wire rack.

When cool enough to handle, transfer the fillets to a large bowl and mash with a fork. Add the bread crumbs, mayonnaise, bell peppers, onions, mustard, pepper, cumin, coriander, and basil. Mix well and shape into 6 cakes. Place on a waxed paper lined baking sheet and cover with plastic wrap. Refrigerate at least 30 minutes or up to 4 hours.

Place the oil in a large skillet over medium-high heat. Place the flour in a shallow dish and dredge the cakes, shaking off the excess. Fry 3 to 4 minutes on each side or until golden brown. Serve warm with cocktail sauce.

**Note:** If you are in a rush, freeze the prepared cakes for 15 minutes to firm them up before frying in the hot oil.

# Southern Catfish Cakes

## Makes 6 servings

4 (5-ounce) catfish fillets

$1/2$ teaspoon salt

$1/4$ cup fresh breadcrumbs

$1/4$ cup mayonnaise

2 tablespoons finely chopped red bell peppers

1 green onion, chopped

1 tablespoon Dijon mustard

1 teaspoon black pepper

$1/2$ teaspoon ground cumin

$1/2$ teaspoon ground coriander

$1/4$ teaspoon dried basil

3 tablespoons canola or vegetable oil

$1/3$ cup all-purpose flour

Cocktail sauce

# Shrimp-Stuffed Catfish Rolls

**Makes 6 servings**

4 (7- to 8-ounce) catfish fillets

1 teaspoon plus 1 tablespoon lemon juice, divided

1/2 teaspoon black pepper

8 slices bacon

1 cup fresh breadcrumbs

3 tablespoons cream cheese, softened

2 tablespoons finely chopped onions

1 tablespoon dried parsley

1 teaspoon dried thyme

1/4 teaspoon salt

1/4 teaspoon white pepper

1/4 pound small or cocktail shrimp, peeled

**This recipe is catfish dressed for success. It's an exhibit of how fancy catfish can become when a little imagination comes into the picture. Although it looks like a special-occasion dinner, it's easy to put together, and the oven does the baking work for you.**

Preheat the oven to 350°F.

Evenly sprinkle the top of each fillet with 1 teaspoon of lemon juice and the black pepper. Set aside.

In a large skillet over medium heat, cook the bacon until it is limp, but not crisp, about 4 minutes total. Drain on paper towels and set aside. Pour the pan drippings into the bottom of an 8-inch square baking dish. Spread evenly along the bottom of the pan and set aside.

In a medium bowl, combine the breadcrumbs, cheese, onions, parsley, thyme, salt, and pepper. Flip the fillets over and spread the breadcrumb mixture evenly on the back side. Sprinkle evenly with the shrimp.

Carefully roll up, jelly-roll-style. Wrap each fillet with 2 slices of bacon and secure with a wooden pick. Place seam side down in the prepared baking dish. Sprinkle with the remaining lemon juice. Bake 25 minutes or until the fish flakes easily with a fork. Remove and discard the wooden picks before serving. Serve hot.

Serve these sandwiches for a casual porch dinner after dangling a fishing pole in the water all day. All it needs is a simple green salad and a glass of dry white wine to end a leisurely day just right.

∾

In a large skillet over medium heat, melt the butter. As soon as it begins to foam, add the onions and garlic and sauté 2 minutes. Add the shrimp, wine, lemon juice, Cajun seasoning, and pepper. Cook 4 to 5 minutes or until the shrimp turn pink, stirring occasionally.

Stir in the dill and parsley. Place the toasted roll halves on four individual serving plates. Spoon 1 cup of the shrimp mixture over each roll and drizzle with any lingering pan juices. Serve immediately.

**Note:** You can also serve the shrimp mixture over hot cooked rice instead of rolls, if desired.

# Open-Faced Cajun Shrimp Sandwiches

**Makes 4 servings**

1/2 cup (1 stick) unsalted butter

1/3 cup chopped green onions

2 garlic cloves, minced

2 pounds large shrimp, peeled and deveined

2 tablespoons dry white wine

1 teaspoon lemon juice

1/4 teaspoon Cajun seasoning

1/4 teaspoon black pepper

1 tablespoon chopped fresh dill

1 tablespoon chopped fresh parsley

2 French rolls, split lengthwise and toasted

# Bayou Crawfish Casserole

**Makes 8 to 10 servings**

6 cups sliced yellow squash

2 cups water

1 purple onion, peeled and chopped

1 green bell pepper, seeded and chopped

1 cup chopped celery

1 garlic clove, minced

1/2 cup (1 stick) unsalted butter

1 egg, beaten

1 cup seasoned dry breadcrumbs

1/3 cup grated Parmesan cheese

1 teaspoon Beau Monde seasoning

1/2 teaspoon salt

1/2 teaspoon black pepper

1/4 teaspoon dried crumbled thyme

1/8 teaspoon cayenne pepper

1/8 teaspoon hot sauce

2 cups peeled crawfish tails

Beau Monde is a ground mixture of salt, onion powder, sugar, and celery seeds that is frequently used to make a Bloody Mary. It's available in the spice section of most grocery stores. Here, it seasons a swallow-your-tongue-good casserole. Crawfish is a tremendous flavor enhancer for this dish. All you need is a side salad and fresh bread for a complete meal.

Preheat the oven to 350°F. Lightly grease a 2-quart casserole dish and set aside.

In a Dutch oven over medium-high heat, bring the squash and water to a boil. Cook 10 minutes, drain and set aside.

Reduce the heat to medium and add the onions, peppers, celery, garlic, and butter. Saute 4 minutes. Remove from the heat and add to the squash, stirring gently. Add the egg, breadcrumbs, cheese, Beau Monde, salt, pepper, thyme, cayenne, hot sauce, and crawfish. Stir to combine. Spoon into the prepared baking pan and bake 30 minutes. Serve warm.

# Rosemary Shrimp

## Makes 4 servings

2 tablespoons unsalted butter

3 tablespoons olive oil

8 garlic cloves, minced

1/2 cup dry white wine

2 tablespoons white wine vinegar

1 tablespoon lemon juice

3 bay leaves

1 teaspoon kosher or sea salt

2 tablespoons chopped fresh rosemary

1 tablespoon chopped fresh oregano

1/2 teaspoon dried crushed red pepper

1 pound medium shrimp, peeled with tails on and deveined

Rosemary sprigs for garnish

**The inspiration for this recipe was shrimp that I threaded on naked rosemary sprigs for the grill. I loved the subtle flavor it added to the shrimp, but wanted to have it when weather kept me from being able to grill outside. This works nicely, and dinner is ready in 10 minutes.**

Melt the butter with the oil in a large skillet over medium-high heat. Add the garlic and sauté 1 minute. Stir in the wine, vinegar, and lemon juice, cooking 1 minute longer. Add the bay leaves, salt, rosemary, oregano, and crushed red pepper. Cook 2 minutes, stirring constantly.

Add the shrimp and cook 4 minutes or just until the shrimp turn pink. Remove the bay leaves and discard. Garnish with the rosemary sprigs and serve as an appetizer or over hot cooked pasta.

Chicken doesn't have the only dibs on that famous version of pot pie. This pork mixture is just as tasty and steps up to the plate when you need something for dinner that's different. A deliciously spiced filling is enveloped in flaky pastry. Yum! You can also substitute ground turkey for the ground pork, if desired.

෴

In a large skillet over medium heat, combine the pork, onions, garlic, carrots, peas, celery, summer savory, salt, and pepper. Cook 7 to 8 minutes, stirring frequently or until the pork is completely done. Break apart any lumps of meat. Sprinkle the top with the flour and stir to incorporate into the pork mixture. Cook another 4 minutes or until the juices are thick. Cool 20 minutes.

Meanwhile, prepare a double quantity of Single-Crust Pie Pastry to make two pie crusts. Place one pastry crust in the bottom of a 9-inch pie plate. Preheat the oven to 425°F. When the filling has cooled, spoon it into the pastry. Top with the remaining pastry, trimming any excess. Press the edges together and crimp as desired.

Brush the pastry top with the milk. Cut 3 steam vents in the top crust with a sharp paring knife. Bake 30 minutes or until golden brown. Let stand 10 minutes before slicing and serving with chutney.

# Spiced Pork Pot Pie

**Makes 6 servings**

1 pound ground pork

1 yellow onion, peeled and chopped

2 garlic cloves, minced

2 carrots, peeled and grated

1 cup fresh green peas

1 celery stalk, finely chopped

3/4 teaspoon dried summer savory or thyme

1 teaspoon salt

1/2 teaspoon black pepper

4 1/2 tablespoons all-purpose flour

2 recipes Single-Crust Pie Pastry (page 191)

1 tablespoon milk

Chutney (for serving)

When the grill finally gets pulled out for the summer, you'll have all the necessary equipment for this recipe. The tomatoes and onions coming in from the garden and hitting the market give it a farm-fresh taste. Add corn on the cob and you've got a summer feast!

❧

Rub the pork slices with the pepper and oregano. Cover and refrigerate at least 30 minutes.

Place the oil in a large saucepan over medium heat. Add the onions and sauté until tender, about 5 minutes. Reduce the heat to low and add the tomatoes, garlic, basil, salt, and fennel seeds. Cook 45 minutes or until thick and bubbly, stirring occasionally.

Prepare the grill by piling the charcoal on one side, leaving the other side empty. For gas grills, light only one side. Place the pork on the grate over the unlit side. Cover and grill 30 minutes (turning halfway through) or until a meat thermometer registers 155°F. Let rest for 3 minutes and serve immediately with the warm tomato marmalade.

# Grilled Pork Loin with Fresh Tomato Marmalade

## Makes 4 servings

4 pork loin slices (about 1 1/2 inches thick)

1 teaspoon black pepper

1 teaspoon dried oregano

1 tablespoon vegetable oil or bacon drippings

1 yellow onion, peeled and chopped

4 ripe tomatoes, peeled and chopped

2 garlic cloves, minced

3 tablespoons minced fresh basil

1/2 teaspoon salt

1/2 teaspoon fennel seeds

# Spinach-Stuffed Pork Roll

**I usually make this dish with leftover steamed spinach from my garden or after a much-needed trip to the local farmers' market. You can use frozen as a substitute, but make sure you thaw and drain it well.**

### Makes 8 to 10 servings

1 (3-pound) boneless pork loin
1/2 pound ground mild or hot Italian sausage
1/2 cup cooked spinach
1/2 cup slivered almonds, toasted
1/4 cup plain dry breadcrumbs
1 egg
2 tablespoons minced fresh parsley
4 garlic cloves, minced
1 teaspoon dried thyme, divided
1 tablespoon olive oil
1 teaspoon black pepper

Soak three (9-inch) pieces of kitchen twine in water for one hour.

Preheat the oven to 350°F. Lightly grease a shallow roasting pan and set aside.

Make a lengthwise slit down the center of the pork that comes to 1/2 inch from the bottom. Lay the pork open and cover with heavy-duty plastic wrap. With a meat mallet, flatten the pork slightly. Remove and discard the plastic wrap and set the pork aside.

In a large bowl, combine the sausage, spinach, almonds, breadcrumbs, egg, parsley, garlic, and 1/2 teaspoon of the thyme. Mix well and spread over the flattened pork. Roll the pork jelly-roll-style and place the seam side down on the prepared pan. Tie with kitchen twine to secure the pork rolls. Brush with the oil and sprinkle with the remaining thyme and pepper.

Bake 2 to 2 1/2 hours or until a meat thermometer inserted in the center registers 160°F. Let stand 10 minutes. Snip off the kitchen twine and discard before slicing the pork in 1 inch slices and serving warm.

I truly love canned beets and make a batch every year from the local roots I purchase at the farmers' market. Then I can enjoy these delicious little crunchy sandwiches for months. They are perfect for lunch with a salad or soup, or slice into fingerlike slivers and serve them as appetizer sandwiches.

# Sassy Pecan and Beet Sandwiches

**Makes 4 sandwiches**

1 (8-ounce) package cream cheese, softened

1/2 cup coarsely chopped toasted pecans

1/4 cup canned beets, drained

2 tablespoons orange juice

8 slices white sandwich bread

Place the cheese, pecans, beets, and juice in the bowl of a food processor. Puree until smooth. Transfer to a covered container and refrigerate at least 1 hour before serving.

Meanwhile, remove the outer crust from slices of white sandwich bread. Using decorative cutters or 2-inch rounds, cut the bread into the desired shapes. Spread the beet mixture on the bread slices and top with the corresponding shape. Serve cold or at room temperature.

**Note:** Sandwiches can be made up to 1 hour ahead and refrigerated until ready to serve.

# Chicken Croquettes with Cherry Tomato Puree

**Makes 6 to 8 appetizer servings or 3 to 4 main dish servings**

2 cups cooked chicken, cut in 1/4-inch pieces

2 tablespoons chopped cilantro

1/4 cup plain dry breadcrumbs

1/4 cup mayonnaise, sour cream, or yogurt cheese

4 tablespoons all-purpose flour

3/4 teaspoon kosher salt, divided

1/2 teaspoon black pepper, divided

15 large cherry tomatoes

1/2 small yellow onion, peeled and cut into small wedges

2 tablespoons olive oil

2 garlic cloves, minced

1 cup plain cornmeal

4 tablespoons vegetable oil

**This recipe is fun to make and serve. The cakes have a marvelous texture, accented by a sauce of roasted cherry tomatoes and onions. I particularly like the combination served over mixed salad greens with roasted sweet corn kernels as the garnish.**

~

In a large bowl, combine the chicken, cilantro, breadcrumbs, and mayonnaise. Add the flour 1 tablespoon at a time until the mixture holds up well and is not too loose. Season with 1/2 teaspoon of the salt and 1/4 teaspoon of the pepper. Cover and refrigerate at least 1 hour.

Preheat the oven to 400°F. Remove the chicken mixture from the refrigerator 30 minutes before making the cakes.

Meanwhile, place the tomatoes and onions in a single layer in a lightly greased jelly-roll pan. In a small bowl, whisk together the olive oil, garlic, and the remaining salt and pepper. Sprinkle over the vegetables. Roast 15 minutes or just until the tomatoes begin to split.

Set aside to cool 10 minutes. When cool, place in a food processor or blender and puree until smooth. Adjust the seasonings if necessary, cover, and set aside.

Divide the chilled chicken mixture and form into 6 to 8 cakes at least 1/2-inch thick. Place the cornmeal in a shallow dish and dredge the cakes in the cornmeal.

Heat the vegetable oil in a large skillet over medium-high heat until hot. Add the cakes and cook 8 to 10 minutes or until golden brown on both sides, turning once. Serve immediately with the cherry tomato puree.

Forget your childhood nightmares of having chicken livers for dinner. This dish will change your mind. When quickly sautéed, chicken livers make an incredible dinner paired with the sweet corn sauce. Your mind will be forever changed about how marvelous this unique cut can be. The corn sauce is equally delicious spooned over roasted pork or grilled fish.

# Quick Sautéed Chicken Livers with Fresh Corn Sauce

❧

In a medium saucepan over low heat, combine the corn, cream, and $1/2$ teaspoon of the salt. Cook 22 to 25 minutes, stirring frequently until thickened.

Meanwhile, in a large skillet over medium heat, melt the butter. When hot and starting to foam, add the shallots and cook 3 to 4 minutes or until limp and golden brown.

Add the livers and increase the heat to high. Sauté 5 minutes, turning to evenly brown. Do not overcook. Drain on paper towels and season with the remaining salt and the pepper. Serve warm with generous portions of the corn sauce for dipping.

**Makes 4 servings**

2 cups fresh sweet corn kernels

2 cups whipping cream

1 teaspoon salt, divided

4 tablespoons unsalted butter

4 shallots, peeled and finely chopped

1 pound chicken livers

$1/2$ teaspoon black pepper

# Confetti Chicken Salad

**Makes 6 servings**

1 cup chicken stock

2/3 cup bulgur wheat

2 cups cooked chicken, chopped

1/2 cup diced celery

1/2 cup chopped tomatoes

1/2 cup chopped purple onions

2 tablespoons lemon juice

1 tablespoon olive oil

1 teaspoon Dijon mustard

1/2 teaspoon garlic salt

1/2 teaspoon black pepper

3 large red bell peppers,
seeded and halved

**The beautiful colors in this salad make it dance on the plate. It's served in red bell pepper halves because I can't seem to get enough of their sweet flavor as they ripen each summer. It's a very "lady's lunch" type of meal or great when you want something light for dinner.**

Bring the stock to a boil in a small saucepan over medium-high heat. Stir in the bulgur wheat and immediately remove from the heat. Cover and let stand 30 minutes.

Meanwhile, gently combine the chicken, celery, tomatoes, and onions in a large mixing bowl. In a separate small bowl, whisk together the juice, oil, mustard, salt, and pepper. Pour over the chicken mixture, stirring to coat.

Drain the bulgur wheat if necessary and fluff with a fork. Combine with the chicken mixture, stirring gently. Cool to room temperature, refrigerate, or serve immediately in the pepper halves.

# Roasted Chicken Pecan Salad

This is a unique twist on a Southern classic! I like to roast the chicken the day before I plan to serve it. Make sure you give the finished recipe plenty of time to rest in the refrigerator before dishing it out to your guests. This lets the flavors meld and marry.

✎

**Makes 6 servings**

1 cup pecan halves, broken in half lengthwise

1 whole roasted chicken, skin and bones removed, cut into bite-size pieces

6 green onions, thinly sliced

2 celery stalks, thinly sliced

2 medium Fuji or Golden Delicious apples, cored, peeled, and diced

5 tablespoons golden raisins

1 tablespoon chopped fresh oregano

1/2 teaspoon salt

1/2 teaspoon black pepper

1/2 cup mayonnaise

3 tablespoons sour cream

1/4 cup cider vinegar

Preheat the oven to 350° F. Spread the pecans in a single layer on an ungreased baking sheet. Roast about 10 minutes or until fragrant, stirring halfway through. Cool on a wire rack.

Meanwhile, combine the chicken, onions, celery, apples, raisins, and oregano in a large mixing bowl. Sprinkle with the salt and pepper. Stir in the pecans.

In a small bowl, combine the mayonnaise, sour cream, and vinegar. Add the dressing to the chicken mixture and toss to combine evenly.

Cover and refrigerate at least 2 hours before serving.

## Indianola Pecan House

Wheeler Timbs
1013 Highway 82 East
Indianola, Mississippi 38751
(662) 887-5420 or 1-800-541-6252
E-mail: pecan@pecanhouse.com
Website: www.pecanhouse.com
Consumer Experience: General store, purchase online

*E*ver since I can remember, the Indianola Pecan House has been my source for purchasing pecans. And the nuts themselves have always been my go-to gift for hostesses who entertain me, because they are versatile, cherished, and uniquely Southern.

For 30 years, the Timbs family has been serving my family with all things pecan. I love that the Indianola Pecan House will shell excess supplies from trees in your own backyard. If you aren't lucky enough to have trees of your own, they have whole nuts that are unshelled and the best value you'll find anywhere. I buy them in 10-pound bags and shell them as I need them for recipes.

But when I want something special, I go for their gourmet packages that are as unique as Southern belles. I am crazy about their mesquite-roasted pecans, followed closely by the garlic roasted pecan halves. Everything is available online, by the way, so you have no excuse not to become acquainted with them yourself. You will not be able to pull your hand away from the numerous savory pecan packages, unless your taste buds are ready for something on the sweet side.

Their original praline pecans can cover you for any occasion from Valentine's Day through Christmas stockings. As much as I adore their chocolate-covered pecans, I am a forever fan of those covered in butterscotch. They are insanely good and a reason to shop there even if you have dozens of pecan trees surrounding your home.

# Skillet Thighs

Makes 6 servings

3 tablespoons olive oil, divided

6 large chicken thighs with skin

1 teaspoon salt

1 teaspoon black pepper

3/4 pound button or cremini mushrooms, quartered

3 cups grape tomatoes

1/2 cup dry red wine

3 garlic cloves, minced

1 teaspoon chopped fresh rosemary

1/4 cup chopped fresh basil

**This dish will change the way you shop for chicken. The thighs are moist, economical, and a delicious cross between white and dark meat. All you need to complete this meal are thick slices of garlic bread.**

Heat 2 tablespoons of the oil in a large skillet over medium-high heat. Sprinkle the chicken with the salt and pepper and add to the hot skillet. Sauté 5 minutes on each side. Transfer the chicken to a large bowl.

Add the mushrooms to the skillet. Sauté until wilted, about 4 minutes. Add the mushrooms to the chicken bowl and any pan drippings. Add the remaining oil to the skillet. When hot, add the tomatoes, wine, garlic, and rosemary. Cover and reduce the heat to medium. Cook 5 minutes.

Using a potato masher, crush half of the tomatoes in the skillet. Return the chicken and mushrooms to the skillet and reduce the heat to medium-low. Simmer uncovered 20 minutes.

With tongs, place the chicken on a platter. Stir the basil into the sauce. Adjust the seasoning if necessary and spoon over the chicken. Serve warm.

# What a Catch! Fish Cakes

### Makes 8 servings

2 pounds cooked fish fillets (trout, tilapia, snapper, or the fish of your choice)

3 eggs, lightly beaten

3 tablespoons cream

1 tablespoon Dijon mustard

2 teaspoons Creole or Cajun seasoning

1 teaspoon Worcestershire sauce

1/4 teaspoon cayenne pepper

1/4 teaspoon black pepper

1/2 cup mayonnaise

1 green onion, chopped

2 tablespoons chopped fresh parsley

1 cup crushed saltine crackers

1 cup plain dry breadcrumbs

4 tablespoons unsalted butter, divided

1/4 cup vegetable oil, divided

**It's hard not to make a platter full of fish, and typically, there are leftovers. In true Southern fashion, they need a transformation before being placed before your family again. Serve these delicious fish cakes with tartar or cocktail sauces, flavored mayonnaise, ketchup, or just a sprinkling of fresh lemon juice.**

In a mixing bowl, flake the fish with a fork. Add the eggs, cream, mustard, seasoning, Worcestershire, cayenne, pepper, mayonnaise, onions, and parsley. Stir until well blended. Fold in the cracker crumbs. Cover and refrigerate 1 hour.

Place the breadcrumbs in a shallow dish. Heat half of the butter and half of the oil in a large skillet over medium-high heat.

Shape the fish mixture into 8 large cakes or patties and dredge in the breadcrumbs. Fry half of the cakes 3 to 4 minutes on each side or until golden. Drain on paper towels and repeat with the remaining butter, oil, and cakes. Serve warm.

**These are flounder fillets with an attitude that shows off sunny Florida at its best. An herb-filled rice mixture is rolled into the fillets to make a marvelous presentation. The fish is topped off with a citrus sauce that is exceptional. If desired, you can substitute grouper, halibut, or tilapia for the flounder.**

❧

Preheat the oven to 350°F. Lightly grease a 13 x 9-inch baking dish and set aside.

In a mixing bowl, combine the rice, carrots, parsley, dill, salt, pepper, and 1 tablespoon of the melted butter. Mix well and spoon about 3 tablespoons of the mixture onto one side of each fillet. Carefully roll up and secure with a wooden pick. Place in the prepared dish and repeat with the remaining fillets and filling.

Brush another tablespoon of the melted butter over the top of each roll. Bake 22 to 25 minutes or until the fish flakes easily with a fork.

Meanwhile, place the remaining butter in a small saucepan over medium heat. In a small bowl, whisk together the orange juice, lemon juice, and cornstarch until smooth. Stir into the butter and whisk constantly until the mixture is thick and bubbly, around 5 minutes. Do not allow the mixture to boil. Serve the sauce spooned over the hot flounder rolls.

# Well-Dressed Flounder Rolls

**Makes 6 servings**

3/4 cup cooked white rice

1/4 cup shredded carrots

1 1/2 teaspoons chopped fresh parsley

1 1/2 teaspoons chopped fresh dill

1/4 teaspoon salt

1/4 teaspoon white pepper

4 tablespoons unsalted butter, melted and divided

6 flounder fillets

1 1/2 cups orange juice

1/4 cup lemon juice

1 1/2 tablespoons cornstarch

I love lamb and always have. Fresh supplies should only be kept in the refrigerator up to 3 days before using. That is never a concern of mine because I use it immediately. Southern vegetables decorate these skewers and make this a complete meal-on-a-stick.

❧

Place the lamb in a large heavy duty zip-top plastic bag. In a mixing bowl, whisk together the onions, garlic, wine, oil, cumin seeds, salt, rosemary, and black pepper. Pour over the lamb and massage to evenly coat. Refrigerate at least overnight or 8 hours and up to 24 hours.

Preheat the broiler and lightly grease a broiler rack. Set aside.

Remove the meat from the marinade and discard the marinade. Alternate the meat, tomatoes, and bell peppers on skewers. Place on the rack and broil 6 minutes. Turn and broil 5 to 6 minutes longer or to the desired degree of doneness. Serve warm.

# Meal-on-a-Stick Lamb Kabobs

**Makes 8 servings**

1 (2 1/2-pound) boned leg of lamb, cut into 1-inch cubes

1 large white onion, peeled and chopped

1 garlic clove, minced

1/2 cup dry red wine

1/2 cup vegetable oil

1 teaspoon cumin seeds

1 teaspoon kosher or sea salt

1 teaspoon chopped fresh rosemary

1 teaspoon black pepper

1 pint cherry tomatoes

3 green bell peppers, seeded and cut into 1-inch squares

# Special-Occasion Stuffed Eggplant

## Makes 4 servings

2 large eggplants

1 tablespoon olive oil

4 tablespoons unsalted butter

2 shallots, peeled and chopped

2 garlic cloves, minced

1 pound lump crabmeat

2 tablespoons fresh chopped parsley

1/2 teaspoon kosher salt

1/4 teaspoon black pepper

1/4 cup dry seasoned breadcrumbs

2 tablespoons grated Parmesan cheese

I love to make this dish on special occasions because the crab gives ordinary eggplant a luxurious texture and taste. Eggplant is a member of the nightshade family and is related to tomatoes and potatoes. Peak supplies hit the market in the late summer, before frost kills the sun-loving plants.

Preheat the oven to 350°F. Cut each eggplant in half lengthwise and brush the cut ends with the oil. Place the cut sides down on a jelly-roll pan and bake 30 minutes. Cool on a wire rack. When cool enough to handle, scoop out the pulp and set aside. Return the shells to the jelly-roll pan with the cut side up.

In a large skillet over medium-high heat, melt the butter. As soon as it begins to foam, add the shallots and sauté 4 minutes. Add the garlic and eggplant pulp. Cook 2 minutes longer.

Stir in the crab, parsley, salt, and pepper. Stuff into the reserved eggplant shells. Sprinkle the tops evenly with the breadcrumbs and cheese. Bake 25 to 27 minutes or until golden brown. Serve warm.

While ground beef is the standard for adding fulfill-ment to chili, it is replaced by a healthy-as-can-be meat substitute. Thanks to quick-cooking lentils, you can have this dish ready to serve at a moment's notice.

∽

Heat the oil in a Dutch oven over medium heat. Add the onions and sauté 2 minutes. Add the garlic and sauté 1 minute longer.

Stir in the chili powder, cumin, oregano, cayenne, stock, len-tils, and tomato puree. Bring to a boil and reduce the heat to low. Simmer, covered, 40 minutes or until the lentils are tender. If necessary, add more stock or water.

Stir in the salt, pepper, and green onions. Serve in warm bowls with a garnish of fresh parsley leaves.

**Note:** This chili can be made up to two days ahead and gently reheated. Leftovers can be frozen up to three months.

# Spiced Lentil Chili

**Makes 4 servings**

2 teaspoons vegetable oil

1/2 cup chopped purple onions

2 garlic cloves, minced

2 tablespoons chili powder

1 tablespoon ground cumin

1 teaspoon dried oregano

1/4 teaspoon cayenne pepper

4 cups vegetable stock

1 cup dried lentils

1/2 cup pureed tomatoes

1/2 teaspoon salt

1/4 teaspoon black pepper

1/2 cup chopped green onions

Fresh parsley for garnish

# Divine from the Vine Tomato Sauce

No adornments are necessary for this sauce that features fresh tomatoes at their finest. I make large pots of this sauce every year when my husband brings armloads of fresh tomatoes into the kitchen. It's quick and full of fresh tomato flavor. I typically freeze most of the excess, but it also preserves well canned.

**Makes 3 cups**

1 tablespoon olive oil
3 garlic cloves, minced
2 shallots, peeled and chopped
4 cups peeled, seeded, and chopped tomatoes
1 cup dry red wine
1 cup chicken or vegetable stock
1/2 teaspoon kosher salt
1/2 teaspoon black pepper

Heat the oil in a large saucepan over medium-high heat. Add the garlic and shallots. Sauté 2 minutes; then add the tomatoes and wine. Cook 10 minutes, stirring occasionally. Add the stock and cook 10 minutes longer.

Using an immersion blender, puree until smooth (or cool slightly and puree in a regular blender). Reduce the heat to medium and add the salt and pepper. Simmer 10 minutes more. Serve over hot cooked pasta.

**Note:** Sauce can be cooled and frozen up to 6 months or canned in a hot water bath for 35 minutes for pints and 40 minutes for quarts.

A pot pie is one of my favorite rainy Sunday comfort foods. This recipe takes advantage of frozen puff pastry to make the preparation as easy as . . . pie!

❧

Preheat the oven to 375°F. Lightly grease a 9- or 10-inch-deep dish pie plate and set aside.

In a large skillet over medium heat, melt the butter. As soon as it foams, add the leeks and cook 3 minutes. Sprinkle with the flour and cook, stirring constantly, for 3 minutes longer to reduce the starchy flavor.

Stir in the stock and bring to a boil, stirring constantly. Remove from the heat and add the chicken, hash browns, carrots, parsley, salt, pepper, and paprika. Cover and set aside.

On a lightly floured surface, roll out each puff pastry sheet into a 12 x 10-inch rectangle. Fit one sheet into the bottom of the prepared dish. Spoon the chicken mixture into the pastry. Top with the remaining pastry facing the opposite direction. Fold the edges under and press with the tines of a fork to seal to the bottom crust. Whisk the egg with a table-spoon of water and brush generously over the top.

Bake on the lower oven rack 55 to 60 minutes or until golden brown. Let stand 10 minutes before serving.

# Easy Crust Chicken Pot Pie

**Makes 6 to 8 servings**

7 tablespoons unsalted butter

2 leeks, sliced

1/2 cup all-purpose flour

1 (14.5-ounce) can low sodium chicken stock

3 cups chopped cooked chicken

1 1/2 cups frozen hash browns with peppers and onions

1 cup chopped carrots

1/3 cup chopped fresh parsley

1/2 teaspoon garlic or seasoned salt

1/2 teaspoon black pepper

1/4 teaspoon paprika

1 (17.3-ounce) package frozen puff pastry, thawed

1 egg

# Winter Solace Chicken and Dumplings

It's cold outside, and your insides could use a little warm pick-me-up. Along comes the old-fashioned standard of chicken and dumplings. In less than an hour, you've got exactly what you need to get through any kind of weather. The aroma it creates will serve as the dinner bell to get your family to the table.

❧

In a large Dutch oven over medium-high heat, stir together the stock, chicken, soup, poultry seasoning, and pepper. Bring to a boil, reduce the heat to low, and simmer, stirring occasionally for 15 minutes.

Meanwhile, make the dumplings by combining the flour, baking powder, and salt in a mixing bowl. In a separate bowl, whisk together the milk and oil. Gradually add to the flour mixture, stirring until moistened.

Drop tablespoons of the dumpling dough onto the surface of the chicken mixture. Cover and cook another 15 minutes. Garnish with the parsley and serve hot.

**Makes 4 to 6 servings**

1 (32-ounce) carton low sodium chicken stock

1 (14-ounce) carton low sodium chicken stock

3 cups (1 1/2 pounds) shredded cooked chicken

1 (10.75-ounce) can cream of celery soup

1/4 teaspoon poultry seasoning

1/4 teaspoon black pepper

2 cups all-purpose flour

4 teaspoons baking powder

1/4 teaspoon salt

1 cup milk

1/4 cup vegetable oil

1/3 cup chopped fresh parsley

## Live Oak Farms

Chuck and Allison Schaum
230 Sam Davis Road
Woodruff, South Carolina 29388
(864) 991-9839
E-mail: Allison@liveoakfarmsllc.com
Website: www.liveoakfarmsllc.com
Consumer Experience: Tour and farm store

If you think all beef is the same, you are mistaken. I am a huge pastured, grass-fed beef fan, and it only took one bite for me to realize what I had been missing. The depth of flavor found in pastured beef is rich and natural. By comparison, it is completely different from the meat of those animals passing through feedlots. Think of a nice glass of dry red wine versus a glass of grape juice.

That's why I admire ranchers like Chuck and Allison Schaum, who dedicate themselves to providing top-quality meats to their community. Veer off exit 35 from I-26 in South Carolina. Live Oak Farms is the 80-acre home to heritage breeds of beef, in addition to lambs, turkeys, chickens, and goats. All the animals are raised without using growth hormones or antibiotics. But the main difference is what the animals are fed. Trust me: you can actually taste the difference.

A trolley tour of Live Oak Farms is worth the investment of your time, and you can go there Monday through Saturday. I like the horse-pulled trolley! You'll get a head full of knowledge on the animal breeds and see the draft horses at work. A plus is the organic produce the Schaums grow, and the milk, butter, cheese, and ice cream products that are truly farm fresh.

Give it a try. Stop by Live Oak Farms, and purchase meat that was raised the way generations before us did . . . naturally, in pastures owned and operated by your neighbors.

# Traditional Southern Pot Roast

**This recipe takes some planning, but the result is a fork-tender piece of meat that is full of fabulous flavor. It may seem tedious, but it's worth every step. Once the stovetop work is complete, let the oven bathe the meat and vegetables in a luscious wine sauce.**

❧

## Makes 8 to 10 servings

1 (6-pound) pot roast or 1 (4-pound) boneless chuck roast

1 tablespoon vegetable oil

2 teaspoons salt

2 tablespoons unsalted butter, divided

1 tablespoon olive oil

1 (2-ounce) slice salt pork

4 yellow onions, peeled and quartered

7 cloves garlic, peeled

3/4 cup dry white wine

1/2 cup chicken stock

1 bay leaf

1/2 teaspoon black pepper

1/2 teaspoon dried crushed thyme

5 carrots, halved

3 turnips, peeled and quartered

1 leek, halved lengthwise

12 small Yukon gold potatoes

Rub the roast with oil and sprinkle with the salt. With your hands, rub the salt into the meat. Refrigerate, uncovered, overnight.

Preheat the oven to 275°F. In a large skillet over medium heat, heat one tablespoon of the butter and the olive oil. When hot, add the beef and salt pork. Deeply brown on all sides 4 to 5 minutes on each side for the roast and about half that time for the salt pork.

Transfer both to a large platter and drain most of the fat from the skillet, leaving behind any browned bits. Add the remaining butter to the pan. As soon as it starts to foam, add the onions and cook 4 to 5 minutes or until they begin to brown. Add the garlic cloves and cook 2 minutes longer.

Stir in the wine and stock, scraping any browned bits from the skillet with a wooden spoon. Transfer the onions and liquid to an 8-quart Dutch oven. Place the roast over the onions. Add the salt pork and bay leaf. Sprinkle with the pepper and thyme.

Place a piece of parchment paper over the roast, tucking around the sides. Cover the parchment with a piece of aluminum foil in the same manner. Cover with the lid and bake on the center rack for 3 hours.

Remove from the oven and lift off the lid, foil, and parchment paper. Tuck the carrots, turnips, leeks, and potatoes around the beef. Cover again with the parchment paper, foil, and the lid. Return to the oven and cook 1 hour longer or until the vegetables are tender. Serve warm.

A platter of fried chicken is a necessity for any Southern family get-together, especially in the summer. The brining step should not be skipped because it adds incredible moisture to the chicken. Buttermilk lends a characteristic tang and zip. Plan ahead for this, and the praises you receive will make it worth the effort.

❧

In a large bowl, combine the salt and water. Add the chicken pieces, cover, and refrigerate 8 hours. Drain the brine mixture and pour the buttermilk over the chicken. Refrigerate another 8 hours.

In a large cast iron skillet, melt the lard over medium-high heat. Meanwhile, drain the chicken from the buttermilk. In a medium bowl, combine the flour, seasoned salt, and pepper. Dredge the chicken in the flour mixture, shaking to remove any excess flour.

Place the pieces in the hot skillet and fry 8 to 10 minutes on each side until the chicken is golden brown. Do not overcrowd the pan. Fry in batches if necessary. Drain on a wire rack placed over paper towels. Serve warm.

# Skillet–Fried Chicken

**Makes 4 to 6 servings**

$1/4$ cup salt

4 cups water

1 (3- to 4-pound) chicken cut into pieces

4 cups buttermilk

1 cup lard or vegetable shortening

1 cup all-purpose flour

1 teaspoon seasoned salt

$1/2$ teaspoon black pepper

# Desserts

Sweet Potato Caramel Pie

Single-Crust Pie Pastry

Cream Cheese Frosting

Orchard-Fresh Peach Cake

Fresh Orange Pound Cake

Fresh Pumpkin Pie

Chocolate Nut Pie

Mixed Chocolate Peanut Clusters

Bourbon Pecan Clusters

Hot Apricots Foster

Zinfandel-Soaked Peaches

Caramel-Drizzled Apple Pie

Spiked Pumpkin Custard

Ring the Doorbell Caramel Apples

Fresh Cherry Cheesecake Topping

Sweet Cherry Dessert Sauce

Sweet on You Persimmon Fudge

Fresh Raspberry Sauce

Perfect Timing Raspberry Soufflé

Damson Ice Cream

Fresh Rhubarb Sauce

Very Vine Dessert

Buttermilk Custard Sauce for Fresh Fruit

Caramel Peach Ice Cream Sauce

Apple Sheet Cake with Caramel Topping

Cherry Pecan Triangles

Lighter-Than-Air Peach Mousse

Coconut Peach Crisp

Under the Stars Blackberry Fool

Caramelized Strawberries with Meringue

Sunny Lemon Granite

Upside-Down Caramelized Nectarines

Plum-Centered Picnic Bars

# Sweet Potato Caramel Pie

**This pie gets a unique twist with a nice caramel topping that replaces traditional whipped cream. The spiced sweet potato filling is like velvet, thanks to the use of evaporated milk.**

❧

### Makes 8 servings

1 recipe Single-Crust Pie Pastry (page 191)

2 eggs

2 cups mashed sweet potatoes

1 (12-ounce) can evaporated milk

3/4 cup sugar

1 teaspoon ground cinnamon

1 1/2 teaspoons pure vanilla extract, divided

1/2 teaspoon ground ginger

1/2 teaspoon ground nutmeg

3 tablespoons dark brown sugar

3 tablespoons light corn syrup

1 tablespoon unsalted butter

Preheat the oven to 425°F.

Prepare the pastry dough. Line a 9-inch pie plate with the pastry, crimp the edges, and set aside.

In a large bowl, combine the eggs, sweet potatoes, milk, sugar, cinnamon, 1 teaspoon of the vanilla, ginger, and nutmeg. Pour into the pastry crust and bake 15 minutes. Reduce the heat to 350°F and bake 25 minutes longer.

In a small saucepan over medium heat, bring the brown sugar, corn syrup, and butter to a boil. Reduce the heat to low and simmer, uncovered, 2 minutes. Remove from the heat and stir in the remaining vanilla.

Drizzle the caramel over the pie and bake 12 to 15 minutes more or until the caramel starts to bubble. Cover the edges with foil if necessary to prevent overbrowning. Cool completely on a wire rack before serving.

The purpose of pastry is to wrap your filling in a flaky crust that is above all else, tender. This is the recipe I always use because it accomplishes just that. Make sure you measure the ingredients accurately and don't overwork the dough.

# Single-Crust Pie Pastry

### Makes 1 crust

1 cup all-purpose flour
1/2 teaspoon salt
1/3 cup vegetable shortening
2 1/2 tablespoons cold water

᠅

In a medium bowl, combine the flour and salt, mixing well. With a pastry blender or two forks, cut in half of the shortening until the mixture is fine textured. Cut in the remaining shortening until the mixture has the consistency of peas. Sprinkle water over the top and stir gently with a fork until the dough leaves the sides of the bowl.

Shape into a ball and then flatten to 1/2-inch thickness, smoothing the edges. Cover with plastic wrap and refrigerate 15 minutes. On a lightly floured surface, roll the dough into an 11-inch round. Loosely roll the dough around the rolling pin and transfer to the pie plate. Do not stretch. Flute the edges with your fingers and set aside.

**Note:** Double the recipe for a two-crust pie, but shape the dough into two equal balls before rolling.

When using this frosting for a fruit cake (such as the Orchard-Fresh Peach Cake), feel free to fold in a half cup of additional chopped fruit to the mixture before spreading on the layers.

# Cream Cheese Frosting

### Makes about 4 cups (enough to frost three 9-inch layers)

12 ounces cream cheese, softened
3/4 cup (1 1/2 sticks) unsalted butter, softened
5 1/4 cups confectioners' sugar
1 1/2 teaspoons pure vanilla extract

᠅

In the bowl of an electric mixer, cream the cream cheese and butter at high speed until fluffy, around 4 minutes. Decrease the mixer speed to low and add the confectioners' sugar and vanilla. Mix well and use immediately.

# Orchard-Fresh Peach Cake

**This layer cake recipe can be used to take you through the entire fruit season. Simply substitute strawberries, nectarines, plums, or apricots for the chopped peaches. Do not use frozen fruit. Only fresh will do.**

**Makes 12 to 14 servings**

1/2 cup (1 stick) unsalted butter
1/2 cup vegetable shortening
2 cups sugar
4 eggs, separated
3 cups all-purpose flour
2 teaspoons baking powder
1/2 teaspoon salt
1/2 cup buttermilk
1/2 cup milk
1/4 cup cream or half-and-half
1 tablespoon pure vanilla extract
3/4 cup finely chopped fresh peaches
Cream Cheese Frosting (page 191)

Preheat the oven to 350°F. Lightly grease and flour three 9-inch round cake pans and set aside.

In the bowl of an electric mixer, cream the butter, shortening, and sugar at high speed for 3 minutes or until fluffy. Reduce the mixer speed to low and add the egg yolks one at a time, mixing well after each addition.

In a separate bowl, combine the flour, baking powder, and salt. Set aside. In another bowl, combine the buttermilk, milk, cream, and vanilla. Beginning and ending with the flour mixture, alternately add the flour and the buttermilk mixture to the batter. Do not overmix. Set aside.

Add the egg whites to the bowl of an electric mixer and whip on high speed until stiff peaks form, around 4 minutes. Gently fold the egg whites and the chopped peaches into the batter. Divide the batter evenly among the prepared cake pans.

Bake 22 to 25 minutes or until a tester inserted in the center comes out clean. Cool on wire racks in the pans, 15 minutes. Remove the cakes from the pans and cool completely before frosting. Note: Garnish the top with fresh peach slices if desired.

Pound cake could be the most perfect summer dessert. It doesn't have to be served warm, but it is fine if it is. It doesn't have to be refrigerated, but it is good that way too. Or serve it at room temperature for a no-fuss summer dessert. This cake is simply fabulous as a light dessert that ends your meal with a citrus punch.

❧

Preheat the oven to 350°F. Grease and flour a 9 x 5-inch loaf pan and set aside.

In the bowl of an electric mixer, cream the butter and sugar at medium-high speed 4 minutes or until light and fluffy. Reduce the mixer speed to medium, and add the eggs one at a time, mixing well between each addition.

In a separate bowl, combine the flour, baking powder, and salt. In another bowl, combine the milk, orange juice, and zest. Beginning and ending with the flour mixture, alternately add the flour and milk to the batter. Transfer the batter to the prepared pan.

Bake 40 to 45 minutes or until a tester inserted in the center comes out clean. Allow the cake to cool in the pan on a wire rack at least 10 minutes. Remove from the pan and cool completely on a wire rack. Just before serving, dust with the confectioners' sugar.

# Fresh Orange Pound Cake

**Makes 8 servings**

$1/2$ cup (1 stick) unsalted butter

$1 1/2$ cups sugar

2 eggs

$1 1/2$ cups all-purpose flour

1 teaspoon baking powder

$1/4$ teaspoon salt

$1/4$ cup milk

$1/4$ cup plus 2 tablespoons freshly squeezed orange juice, divided

$1/2$ teaspoon grated orange zest

$1/3$ cup confectioners' sugar

### Jones Orchard

Henry Jones
6880 Singleton Parkway
Millington, Tennessee 38053
(901) 872-0703 or (901) 872-7974
E-mail: lwjones@jonesorchard.com
Website: http://www.jonesorchard.com
Consumer Experience: Pick your own, farm market, tour,
corn maze, hayrides, haunted woods

Get ready to have a howling good time beginning in September and running through October at Jones Orchard and Corn Maze in Millington, Tennessee. If you like pumpkins, this is the place to be. Everything from sugar and pie pumpkins to the increasingly popular Cinderella types are there for your selection. Want a mammoth one for your yard display? It's there. Do you only need some mini pumpkins for individual servings at your next fall dinner? That's not a problem at Jones Orchard.

Millington is only about 15 miles north of Memphis. Although Jones Orchard is famous for their fall fun, they have mountains of fresh strawberries, plums, and peaches ready for picking throughout the summer.

But in the fall, begin with a trip through a 10-acre corn maze that has an alien-abduction theme. It is cut by a GPS system, so when you are tracking your progress through the map, it's accurate by the inch.

Then head on over to the "Train of Terror" haunted woods featuring live actors. According to owner Henry Jones, the biggest attraction is the farm's signature "Black Hole"—a 20-foot tunnel that spins as you walk and creates a disorienting optical illusion. It's a crazy kind of family fun.

After all that excitement, it's time for a nice, relaxing hayride to the pumpkin patch, where you can pick your own pumpkins right off the vine. It is a full Halloween experience and offers fun for the whole family. And you'll leave with the makings of a fantastic fresh pumpkin pie.

**Forget that tasteless canned pumpkin pie filling at the supermarket. After a fun trip to the local pumpkin patch, only the freshest pumpkin pie will do for your family and friends. If your pumpkin yields more than 3 cups of pureed pumpkin, just freeze the remainder for later and use within 6 months.**

❧

Preheat the oven to 350°F. Line a jelly-roll pan with aluminum foil and set aside.

With a sturdy knife, cut the pumpkin into four large chunks. Remove and discard the seeds and strings. Place the pumpkin, cut side down, on the prepared pan. Roast 45 minutes or until the pumpkin is easily pierced when a knife is inserted in the flesh. Let cool completely on a wire rack.

With a sharp knife, remove the pumpkin rind and discard. Place the pumpkin pulp pieces in the bowl of a food processor. Puree until smooth and measure 3 cups. Reserve any extra for another use.

Preheat the oven to 375°F. Line a 9-inch pie plate with the pastry and crimp the edges with a fork. In a mixing bowl, combine the pumpkin puree, eggs, honey, half-and-half, cinnamon, nutmeg, and salt. Mix until smooth and pour the filling into the prepared shell.

Place the filled pie on a baking sheet and place in the middle of the oven. Bake 55 to 60 minutes or until a tester inserted in the center comes out clean. Cool completely on a wire rack before serving.

# Fresh Pumpkin Pie

**Makes 8 servings**

1 (3-pound) sugar or pie pumpkin

1 recipe Single-Crust Pie Pastry (page 191)

4 eggs, lightly beaten

3/4 cup honey

1 cup half-and-half

1/2 teaspoon ground cinnamon

1/2 teaspoon ground nutmeg

1/2 teaspoon salt

## Chaney's Dairy Barn

Carl and Debra Chaney
9191 Nashville Road
Bowling Green, Kentucky 42101
(270) 843-5567
E-mail: chaneyinfo@yahoo.com
Website: www.chaneysdairybarn.com
Consumer Experience: Tour, general store, restaurant,
purchase in retail outlets

Farm charm is what pulls you into Chaney's Dairy Barn, and a visit with Carl Chaney is what will keep you there. He weaves his family history in the Jersey cow business into what is a stellar stop on your way through Kentucky.

The farm was originally purchased by his family in 1888 and became a dairy

farm in 1940. Much to the delight of anyone who loves good ice cream, Chaney's Dairy Barn opened in 2003 and has been making people hit the brakes ever since. It's open year-round, and all you have to do is follow the line of vehicles headed that way! The drive there is scenic even though it isn't out of the way.

I first visited Chaney's with my friend Megan. We secretly envied the nice homes that are located close by. Can you imagine living that close to a fantastic ice cream parlor? It would be a kid's dream come true!

Their chocolate milk is nothing short of spectacular, and the restaurant is a popular lunch and dinner hangout. With more than 30 ice cream flavors, it would be difficult to pick a favorite. However, the peach with chunks of real peaches throughout is quite hard to resist and "udderly" incredible!

Whether you find walnuts or pecans on the market, you'll discover that both are right at home in this recipe. It's deliciously rich, and the bit of rum beautifully permeates the entire pie. Don't leave it out!

❧

Preheat the oven to 375°F. Place the pastry in a 9-inch pie plate and crimp the edges with a fork. Set aside.

In a heavy saucepan over medium-low heat, combine the syrup and sugar. Stirring constantly, bring the mixture to a boil. Remove from the heat and add the chocolate and butter. Stir until well blended.

Add 1/2 cup of the hot mixture to the eggs, stirring well. Return the egg mixture to the chocolate mixture and stir well. Add the rum and nuts, stirring just to combine. Pour into the pie pastry.

Place in the oven and immediately reduce the oven temperature to 350°F. Bake 45 to 50 minutes or until a knife inserted in the center comes out clean. Place on a wire rack to cool completely. Serve at room temperature.

# Chocolate Nut Pie

**Makes 8 servings**

1 recipe Single-Crust Pie Pastry recipe (page 191)

1 1/4 cups dark corn syrup

3/4 cup sugar

2 ounces unsweetened chocolate, chopped

4 tablespoons unsalted butter

4 eggs, lightly beaten

1 tablespoon dark rum

2 cups pecan halves or coarsely broken black walnuts

# Mixed Chocolate Peanut Clusters

This is one of those recipes that I've been making so long I'm not sure where I got it. I just know it's easy and impossible not to love. Use it for teacher's gifts, Halloween surprises, or just because the weekend is coming.

**Makes 42 candies**

6 ounces almond bark or white confectioners' coating, chopped
6 ounces semisweet chocolate, chopped
1 1/2 cups whole peanuts without skins

Cover two baking sheets with waxed paper or aluminum foil and set aside.

In the bottom of a double boiler, fill with water to 1 inch below the bottom of the top pan. Set it over medium heat until the water is hot, but not simmering.

Place the almond bark and semisweet chocolate in the top pan of the double boiler and attach a candy thermometer. Place over the hot water and stir constantly until the mixture melts and reaches 85°F. Quickly add the peanuts and stir to evenly coat.

Drop rounded teaspoons of the candy onto the prepared pans. Cool completely and remove from the waxed paper. Transfer to an airtight container for storage.

## Hardy Farms Peanuts

Alex Hardy
1659 Eastman Highway
Hawkinsville, Georgia 31036
(888) 368-NUTS (6887) or (478) 783- 3044
E-mail: info@hardyfarmspeanuts.com
Website: www.hardyfarmspeanuts.com
Consumer Experience: Farm stands, purchase online

Boiled peanuts fall into the love-them-or-leave-them category, with few who are indifferent. I happen to love them, and a trip to middle Georgia always means a stop at one of the 24 Hardy Farms Peanuts roadside stands or sales shacks. You won't drive far and not find one, no matter what time of the year you are driving through.

When I say, "shack," I am not kidding. There is nothing fancy about these outlets, and you won't find shelves full of other trinkets or foods . . . just peanuts straight from the boiling pot. I dare you to make it back to the car without trying one.

Hardy Farms grows 850 acres of peanuts, and green peanuts are harvested from 550 of those acres. (Green peanuts are those pulled right out of the field.) The Hardy family began picking them green in the 1980s. According to Alex Hardy, they begin in March and plant peanuts every week to extend the season. It has been a recipe for success, with the farm producing around 3 million pounds of peanuts this year alone.

Within 15 minutes of digging, the peanuts are picked and sent to the processing shed. There they are washed, graded, blanched (for the ones they freeze), and eventually boiled. The resulting peanuts in the shell are served warm and have just the right amount of saltiness and crunch. You will eat yourself silly and immediately be on the lookout for yet another one of those sales shacks for a drive-by peanut fix.

# Bourbon Pecan Clusters

## Makes 20 candies

60 pecan halves (about 1 pound)

1/3 cup bourbon

26 caramels (about half of a 14-ounce package)

2 tablespoons unsalted butter, divided

4 ounces bittersweet chocolate, chopped

**These candies are easy to make and are a perfect gift for anyone who needs just a little pick-me-up. I've tried all types of spirits in this recipe, and bourbon always wins hands down. Its flavor seems to soak into the pecans best. Store any leftovers in an airtight container in the refrigerator, but bring it to room temperature when you're ready to serve.**

☙

Place the pecans in a shallow bowl and add the bourbon. Let stand 30 minutes, stirring occasionally. Preheat the oven to 350°F.

Drain the pecans and reserve 2 tablespoons of the bourbon. Place the pecans in a single layer in a jelly-roll pan. Roast 10 minutes, stirring halfway through. Cool in the pan 30 minutes on a wire rack.

Remove the pecans from the pan and line the pan with waxed paper. Lightly grease the waxed paper. Place groupings of 3 pecans each on the pan and set aside.

In a saucepan over low heat, combine the caramels, one tablespoon of the butter, and the reserved bourbon. Stir constantly until the caramels melt. Evenly drizzle the caramel over the pecan clusters. Place the pan in the freezer 30 minutes to firm.

In a glass measuring cup, microwave the chocolate and remaining butter on high power for 1 minute or until melted. Stir until smooth. Drizzle chocolate over the clusters. Let stand 30 minutes before serving.

## Hot Apricots Foster

Don't let the lighting procedure of this recipe scare you. It is dramatic, and you'll find it fun once you've tried it. This step is only done after the food is warmed. The correct term is *flambé*, which is the French word for "flaming." Use this apricot version of bananas foster as a topping for vanilla ice cream or pound cake.

❧

In a large skillet over medium heat, melt the butter. Add the apricots and sauté 2 minutes. Stir in the sugar, juice, and cinnamon. Reduce heat to low and simmer 20 minutes, stirring frequently.

Add the liqueur and tilt the pan away from you. Light with a long-handled match and let the flames slowly extinguish. Serve immediately over ice cream or toasted slices of pound cake.

**Makes 6 servings**

4 tablespoons unsalted butter
8 fresh apricots, pitted and thinly sliced
$1/2$ cup sugar
$1/2$ cup orange juice
$1/4$ teaspoon ground cinnamon
$1/4$ cup Grand Marnier or orange liqueur

## Zinfandel-Soaked Peaches

This recipe alone is a great excuse to seek out your local winery. Our neighborhood vineyard gives us value-added agricultural products at their finest. Oh, and you must use fresh peaches for this recipe. The wine seeps into every part of the peach, giving it flavor times ten!

❧

In a large bowl, whisk together the wine and sugar. Add the peaches, cover, and let stand at room temperature 2 hours. Serve over homemade vanilla ice cream.

**Makes 6 servings**

2 cups Zinfandel
2 tablespoons sugar
6 fresh peaches, peeled, pitted, and sliced

# Caramel-Drizzled Apple Pie

**Makes 8 servings**

1 recipe Single-Crust Pie Pastry (page 191)

1/2 cup caramel syrup, divided

6 cups peeled and sliced Granny Smith apples

1 teaspoon lemon juice

1 teaspoon pure vanilla extract

1 1/3 cups chopped pecans, toasted and divided

1/3 cup packed light brown sugar

3 tablespoons plus 1/4 cup sugar, divided

4 teaspoons ground cinnamon

1 tablespoon cornstarch

3/4 cup all-purpose flour

6 tablespoons unsalted butter

I'm not sure which is harder to handle: smelling this pie bake and waiting for it to come out of the oven or waiting for it to cool so you can have a slice. I like to use sweetly tart Granny Smith apples for pie making. They hold up well in cooking without losing their shape like other apples, such as Jonathans, tend to do. The caramel sauce is on the bottom of the apples and drizzled over the top for a double dose!

Preheat the oven to 350°F. Line a 9-inch pie plate with the pastry. Drizzle 1/4 cup of the caramel syrup over the bottom and set aside.

In a large mixing bowl, toss the apples with the juice and extract. In a separate bowl, combine 2/3 cup of the pecans, brown sugar, 3 tablespoons of the sugar, cinnamon, and cornstarch. Add to the apples and toss to evenly coat. Place in the pastry shell.

In a small bowl, combine the flour, remaining pecans, and remaining sugar. With a pastry blender or two forks, cut in the butter until the mixture resembles coarse meal. Sprinkle over the apple filling.

Bake 55 to 65 minutes or until the filling is bubbly and the topping is golden brown. Remove from the oven and immediately drizzle with the remaining caramel syrup. Cool completely on a wire rack before cutting and serving.

I love make-ahead desserts, and this one has fall written all over it. The custards bake in a hot water bath that evenly cooks them and yields a soft, smooth texture. Although you can enjoy them warm, I prefer to present them chilled. You can garnish with a sprinkling of ground cinnamon or with whipped cream . . . or both!

❧

Preheat the oven to 325°F. Lightly grease six (6-ounce) ramekins or custard cups. Place in a 13 x 9-inch baking dish and set aside.

In a heavy saucepan over medium heat, combine the half-and-half, cream, and sugar, stirring constantly until the mixture comes to a simmer (do not boil). Remove from the heat and set aside.

In a mixing bowl, combine the eggs, pumpkin, liqueur, zest, ginger, and salt. Whisk until smooth. Gradually whisk 1/2 cup of the hot mixture into the pumpkin mixture. Blend well. Add to the remaining hot mixture and stir constantly until smooth.

Pour evenly into ramekins and add hot water to the baking dish to a depth of one inch. Bake 50 minutes or until a knife inserted in the center comes out clean. Remove the ramekins from the water bath and cool completely on wire racks. Cover and chill at least 2 hours before serving. Garnish with freshly whipped cream if desired.

# Spiked Pumpkin Custard

**Makes 6 servings**

1 cup half-and-half
1/2 cup whipping cream
1/2 cup sugar
3 eggs, beaten
1 cup mashed pumpkin
2 tablespoons Grand Marnier
1 tablespoon grated orange zest
1/4 teaspoon ground ginger
Pinch of salt
Freshly whipped cream for garnish

Don't reserve this recipe for Halloween. Rich, sweet caramel contrasts with the tart apples so well that you'll want to enjoy this goodie through-out the year. It's a fun, unexpected treat to pack in picnic baskets.

∼

Line a baking sheet with waxed paper and set aside. Remove the stems of the apples and discard. Insert the sticks into the stem end of each apple and set aside.

In a heavy saucepan, combine the sugar, milk, shortening, and salt over medium-high heat. Mix well and bring to a boil. Boil 2 minutes, stirring constantly.

Remove from the heat and stir in the extract. Use the whisk attachment on an electric mixer to beat the caramel at medium speed until the mixture thickens and loses its gloss, about 7 minutes.

Dip the apples in the caramel, covering the entire surface. Allow the excess to drip back into the pan. Place on the pre-pared baking sheet to harden at least 1 hour before serving.

**Note:** If any caramel is left over, drizzle over the apples. The apples can be rolled in chopped nuts immediately after dipping in the caramel if desired. You can also drizzle the tops with melted chocolate.

# Ring the Doorbell Caramel Apples

**Makes 6 servings**

6 small or medium Granny Smith or Newtown Pippin apples

6 wooden treat sticks or skewers

2 cups packed light brown sugar

1/2 cup milk

1/2 cup vegetable shortening

1/2 teaspoon salt

1 teaspoon pure vanilla extract

## Orr's Farm Market

Mark and Mike Orr
682 Orr Drive
Martinsburg, West Virginia 25403
(304) 263-1168
E-mail: info@orrsfarmmarket.com
Website: www.orrsfarmmarket.com
Consumer Experience: Pick your own, farm stand, bakery

*I* have loved fresh cherries since I was a little girl. There is something about seeing them hanging on the trees, all ripe and red, that pulls you toward them and beckons you to start picking and nibbling.

I would be hard-pressed to rank sweet or tart cherries as first or second place because I use the two for such different cooking projects. Luckily, Orr's Farm Market in Martinsburg, West Virginia, has them both, so go there in June and try to decide for yourself. They are equally exquisite fruits. The bakery reminds me of my own grandmother's kitchen because of the pie aroma that is no less than intoxicating. The pies are all deep-dish with a flaky, scrumptious crust that is a reminder of home.

This family farm history began in the 1930s when George Orr helped his grandfather on the family fruit farm. By 1954, he had purchased his own 60 acres of farmland, and it has blossomed ever since. You'll find Orr family members and in-laws in every phase of the operation, and it shows in the care you witness around every piece of the business. Today, they have hundreds of acres to lovingly manage.

The farm market has fluid hours that ebb and flow according to the produce season, so check their website regularly for their operating hours. No matter when you go, you can check out their bison herd. It feels as if you have stepped back in time to see them grazing the land. The day I was there, I counted a dozen of these gentle giants lumbering serenely through the pastureland.

Cherries take the spotlight for me, but the Orr family also grows strawberries, pears, apples, peaches, nectarines, and plums.

This topping is equally at home on a chocolate, swirled, or plain cheesecake. Or serve it on toasted slices of pound cake or angel food cake. Kirsch is a clear brandy that is distilled from both the cherry juice and pits. You probably have it on hand for use in fondue recipes, where it sings next to cheese. I have a handheld cherry pitter to make the job of removing the pit a cinch. It is not expensive, and you can find one at any good kitchen store. It is also great for pitting olives.

❧

Heat the butter in a large saucepan over medium-high heat. Add the cherries and sauté 5 minutes. Stir in the sugar and sauté 3 minutes more.

Immediately remove from the heat and add the kirsch and extract. Mix well. Cool to room temperature before use, or refrigerate for later use.

# Fresh Cherry Cheesecake Topping

**Makes 4 cups**

2 tablespoons unsalted butter

5 cups fresh sweet or tart cherries, pitted

3/4 cup sugar

1/2 cup kirsch or cherry brandy

1/2 teaspoon pure almond extract

# Sweet Cherry Dessert Sauce

### Makes 1½ cups

1 pound sweet cherries

⅓ cup sugar

¼ cup kirsch or cherry brandy

2 tablespoons minced crystallized ginger

2 (¼-inch thick) lemon slices, seeded

1 tablespoon cornstarch dissolved in 1 tablespoon water

I've used this sauce in so many ways. Sometimes it's spooned over ice cream. Other times, I use it as a mini-tart filling. It may show up over custard or pudding. In other words, it's versatile, and there's only one pot to wash when you are finished. This recipe spotlights the ease of using cornstarch to thicken sauces.

Combine the cherries, sugar, kirsch, ginger, and lemon slices in a medium saucepan over medium heat. Bring to a boil, reduce the heat to low, and simmer 10 to 12 minutes or until slightly thickened.

Remove the lemon slices and discard. Stir in the cornstarch mixture. Cook and stir until thickened, about 5 minutes. Cool completely.

**Note:** Store leftovers in the refrigerator.

# Sweet on You Persimmon Fudge

**Makes 3 dozen pieces**

6 cups sugar

2 1/2 cups milk

1 cup persimmon pulp

1/2 cup light corn syrup

1/2 cup (1 stick) unsalted butter

1 cup chopped pecans or walnuts

Delicious fudge is always a treat. This one gets a sweet depth from persimmon pulp and a nice crunch from fall nut meats. Persimmons come in two varieties and many sizes, so creating the pulp for this recipe could take between two (large) and ten (small) fruits. For this recipe use the hachiya persimmon, since it's much sweeter than the fuyu variety. Fruits that are not quite ripe (think like you would for peaches) should be kept at room temperature. Refrigerate only those that are ripe and ready to use, but don't wait too long to make this delicious fudge!

Lightly grease an 8-inch square baking pan and set aside.

Grease the sides of a large, heavy saucepan and place over medium heat. Add the sugar, milk, persimmon pulp, syrup, and butter. Cook around 20 minutes or until a candy thermometer registers 230°F, stirring constantly.

Remove from the heat and do not disturb until the temperature drops to 180°F, around 15 minutes. Briskly stir in the pecans with a wooden spoon until the mixture thickens, around 5 minutes. Quickly transfer to the prepared pan and smooth evenly. Cool completely on a wire rack before cutting into squares.

**Note:** Store in an airtight container between layers of waxed paper.

### High Springs Orchard and Bakery

Charles and Jenny Franklin
10804 Northwest State Road 45
High Springs, Florida 32643
(352) 222-1343
E-mail: chuck@highspringsorchard.com
Website: www.highspringsorchard.com
Consumer Experience: Pick your own, farm market, bakery

Some folks don't pick persimmons at the supermarket, much less off the actual tree. But that could change quickly after harvesting and biting into a perfectly ripe persimmon.

Forget the stories of horribly puckered mouths twisted from the astringency of one that wasn't ready to pluck from the branches. Charles and Jenny Franklin at High Springs Orchard will only guide you to rows that are ready for the fruit to be pulled. They know what they are doing and have been growing persimmons for nearly two decades.

In the mid-1990s, they purchased a 28-acre Florida farm and began their dream with a few persimmon trees. Now there are hundreds of them, along with trees loaded with chestnuts, Asian pears, and apples.

Buckets and shears are lined up and ready for customers to use as they venture out to the orchard. You will be surprised at how quickly you have the bucket full. Jenny is determined to turn persimmon skeptics around, even encouraging them to take a bite right there in the orchard. "If they don't like it, they can spit it out," she told me. I have a feeling that happens very rarely, because the tangy yet sweet fruit has a creamy, smooth texture reminiscent of pudding. You will wonder how you ever made it this far in life without them.

Note: Persimmons are available beginning in late September, but High Springs Orchard has other produce ready for picking throughout the spring and summer. Treat yourself to a delicacy from the orchard bakery, open year-round. The Chocolate Butter Cream Cake is to die for!

# Fresh Raspberry Sauce

Raspberries should be married to chocolate! This sauce is terrific over chocolate pudding, chocolate ice cream, or a chocolate pound cake. They are fragile fruits, so if possible, store them in a single layer in the refrigerator. When strawberries are in season, substitute them for the whole raspberries in this recipe.

**Makes 1½ cups**

2 pints fresh raspberries
¼ cup orange juice
2 teaspoons honey

Place the raspberries, orange juice, and honey in the container of a blender or food processor. Puree until smooth. Strain through a fine mesh sieve and discard the solids.

Refrigerate, covered, until ready to serve. Use within 2 days.

## McGarrah Farms

Dennis and Dawn McGarrah
16329 North Old Wire Road
Garfield, Arkansas 72732
(479) 451-8164
E-mail: dennis@mcgarrahfarms.com
Website: www.mcgarrahfarms.com
Consumer Experience: Pick your own, farm market,
purchase in local retail outlets

*A*ccidents can sometimes be a good thing, and my unexpected discovery of McGarrah Farms in Garfield, Arkansas, was one of them. I was on my way to a meeting in the mid-1990s (before the days of GPS), and it was a sticky, hot day in early September. I don't know how I got there, but I somehow found myself in the middle of farm country. To my complete surprise, I was surrounded by loads of fresh raspberries. I had to hit the brakes, and I've been stopping by there ever since on purpose.

There is something aristocratic and regal about fresh raspberries. I didn't grow up enjoying them, but only realized I loved them as an adult. Far too frequently, the price tag kept me at bay, so I made it a point to note exactly when the fresh season started so I could indulge myself in this glorious fruit with abandon.

The Heritage red variety that Dennis and Dawn McGarrah grow is my all-time favorite. These are a perfect blend of sweet and tart, and look the way fresh raspberries are supposed to look . . . red!

Benton County, Arkansas, residents have benefited from Dennis's upbringing for years because he grew up farming with his grandfather. He likes to say he added his children to the mix as soon as they could walk.

The fresh raspberry season begins mid-August and continues through the middle of October. While the McGarrahs also grow delicious strawberries and blackberries, I will forever go there for the raspberries and appreciate getting lost in the Arkansas countryside with each nibble.

Timing is everything with this out-of-the-ordinary dessert. It isn't the type of ending for an everyday meal. Instead, it is the crescendo for an anniversary or birthday celebration, Valentine's Day, or Mother's Day. I like to serve it on New Year's Eve when you are only tied to the clock at midnight! Crème de cassis is a black currant–flavored liqueur, and it is in excellent balance with the tang of raspberries.

# Perfect Timing Raspberry Soufflé

**Makes 6 servings**

2 tablespoons plus $1/2$ cup confectioners' sugar, divided

2 cups fresh raspberries

1 tablespoon crème de cassis

5 egg whites

$1/2$ teaspoon pure almond extract

---

Preheat the oven to 350°F. Lightly grease a 4-cup soufflé dish and sprinkle 2 tablespoons of confectioners' sugar in an even, thin layer around the inside. Place on a baking sheet and set aside.

In a food processor, puree the raspberries, the remaining sugar, and the liqueur. Strain through a fine mesh sieve into a medium bowl and discard the solids.

In the bowl of an electric mixer, whip the egg whites until stiff peaks form. Add the almond extract. Gently fold the puree into the whipped whites just until blended. Spoon into the soufflé dish. Bake 25 to 30 minutes until risen and set. Serve immediately.

# Damson Ice Cream

## Makes 2½ quarts

2⅓ cups plus ¾ cup sugar, divided

3 cups half-and-half

6 egg yolks

½ teaspoon salt, divided

3 cups peeled and quartered damson plums

⅓ cup water

2 tablespoons cornstarch

2 tablespoons unsalted butter, softened

3½ cups heavy whipping cream

4 teaspoons pure vanilla extract

Damsons are a variety of plum that have a yellow-green flesh and are extremely tart. They are small and oval shaped with a dark skin. If you substitute other plums in this recipe, you will need to reduce the sugar, so let taste be your guide. Although this recipe contains eggs, they are cooked into a custard, making this a good, safe recipe for all ages to enjoy.

Fill the bottom pan of a double boiler with 3 inches of water and place over medium heat. Place 2⅓ cups of the sugar, the half-and-half, egg yolks, and ¼ teaspoon of the salt in the top of a double boiler and set over the heating water. Cook around 10 minutes, stirring frequently, until the mixture thickens and coats the back of a spoon. Transfer to a bowl to cool. Cover with plastic wrap, making sure the wrap touches the custard so a film doesn't form on top. Refrigerate until cold, around 2 hours.

In a large saucepan, combine the plums and water over medium-high heat. Bring to a boil and reduce the heat to medium. Simmer 3 minutes.

Meanwhile, in a mixing bowl, combine the remaining sugar, cornstarch, and the remaining salt. Add to the plum mixture and cook 3 minutes longer. Remove from the heat and stir in the butter until completely melted. Add the cream and vanilla extract. Blend well.

Stir into the custard mixture until well combined. Transfer to an ice cream freezer and freeze according to the manufacturer's directions.

# Fresh Rhubarb Sauce

I love the competing and complex flavors in this sauce anchored with fresh spring rhubarb. It is remarkable over toasted pound cake. It is also delightful over roasted pork or turkey.

❧

**Makes 3 cups**

2 cups (1/2-inch pieces) sliced rhubarb
1 (10-ounce) jar seedless raspberry jam or preserves
2/3 cup honey
2 tablespoons cider vinegar
1/8 teaspoon ground cloves

In a heavy saucepan over medium heat, combine the rhubarb, jam, honey, vinegar, and cloves, stirring well to blend. Bring to a boil and reduce the heat to medium-low. Simmer 10 minutes. Cover and set aside to cool at least 30 minutes.

Transfer the rhubarb mixture to the bowl of a food processor and process until smooth. Serve immediately or refrigerate for later use.

# Very Vine Dessert

Want something effortless to serve at your next dinner party for dessert? Seedless grapes rest under a fluffy, only slightly sweet cloud of white. Crunchy, toasted almonds finish it off, and your guests will love it.

❧

**Makes 6 to 8 servings**

3/4 pound red seedless grapes
3/4 pound green seedless grapes
1 (8-ounce) carton sour cream
2 tablespoons plus 1 teaspoon sugar
1 tablespoon light rum
1/4 teaspoon ground cinnamon
1/3 cup chopped almonds, toasted

Cut the grapes in half lengthwise and place in a serving bowl. Set aside.

In a small mixing bowl, whisk together the sour cream, sugar, rum, and cinnamon. Stir until the sugar completely dissolves. Spoon over the grapes. Sprinkle with the almonds and serve immediately.

Ladle this creamy sauce over anything you want and it will fit in just fine. I love to drizzle it over baked meringues or any fresh fruit. You'll find endless reasons to make it and keep it on hand throughout the summer fresh fruit season.

In a heavy saucepan, whisk together the buttermilk, sugar, cornstarch, and egg yolks. Place over medium heat and bring to a boil. Whisk constantly for 1 minute and stir in the vanilla extract. Cool completely and refrigerate until ready to ladle over fresh berries.

# Buttermilk Custard Sauce for Fresh Fruit

**Makes 3 cups**

3 cups buttermilk

3/4 cup sugar

1 tablespoon cornstarch

4 egg yolks, lightly beaten

1 teaspoon pure vanilla extract

Fresh strawberries, blueberries, blackberries, raspberries or a mixture

Pan roasting the peaches deepens the flavor and keeps the sauce from being too sweet.

In a large saucepan over medium-high heat, combine the sugar and water. Cook until the sugar starts to turn golden brown, but do not stir, about 15 minutes.

Add the peaches, rum, and corn syrup and cook about 2 minutes more. Add the butter and cook until melted and smooth. Set aside to cool slightly before serving.

**Tip:** Spoon over vanilla ice cream, plain cheesecake, or toasted angel food cake.

# Caramel Peach Ice Cream Sauce

**Makes 2 1/2 cups**

2 cups sugar

1/2 cup water

4 fresh peaches, peeled, pitted, and diced

1/4 cup dark rum

1/4 cup light corn syrup

2 tablespoons unsalted butter

# Apple Sheet Cake with Caramel Topping

**Makes 16 servings**

2 1/2 cups sugar, divided

4 eggs

1 cup vegetable oil

3 cups all-purpose flour

1 teaspoon baking soda

1 teaspoon salt

3 cups thinly sliced Golden Delicious apples

1 cup chopped pecans or walnuts

1/2 cup packed dark brown sugar

4 tablespoons unsalted butter

1/4 cup evaporated milk

1 teaspoon pure vanilla extract

**Sheet cakes are very popular in the South, thanks to their portability. This moist cake is kept that way with a warm caramel topping that's poured over the luscious cake after it comes out of the oven.**

❧

Lightly grease a 13 x 9-inch baking pan and set aside.

In the bowl of an electric mixer, combine 2 cups of the sugar, eggs, and oil. Beat until well blended.

In a separate bowl, combine the flour, baking soda, and salt. Gradually add to the egg mixture with the mixer speed reduced to low. Gently stir in the apples and pecans.

Spread into the prepared pan. Place in a cold oven and set the oven temperature to 325°F. Bake 55 minutes. Cool in the pan on a wire rack.

Meanwhile, in a small saucepan over medium-high heat, combine the remaining sugar, brown sugar, butter, and evaporated milk. Bring to a boil and cook, stirring constantly 2 minutes. Stir in the vanilla extract. Cool about 10 minutes and pour over the cooled cake. Let stand at least 10 minutes before serving.

## Collins Round Mountain Orchard

Racy and Marcie Garis
159 Mill Pond Road
Conway, Arkansas 72034
(501) 327-0450
Website: www.collinsorchards.com
Consumer Experience: Pick your own, farm market

The first time I met Richard and Barbara Collins, I thought they were the picture everyone should see when they think of farmers. We were at an apple meeting, and I had several days to get to know them. Soon I discovered they were just as lovely on the inside as they were on the outside . . . and boy, did they know how to grow exceptional apples!

Both have since retired, but thankfully, their daughter and son-in-law have followed right along in their footsteps, making Collins Round Mountain Orchard the place to shop for farm-fresh apples beginning in August and continuing into the holiday season.

Now, everyone knows that the type of apple you select should be based on how you are going to use it. That's why you can't go wrong in Conway, Arkansas. When I visited, there were no fewer than seven different varieties to select from, and I was so enthralled by the unique qualities of each, I bought all of them! The mixture of various ones in my pies, apple butters, and jellies was spectacular. It changed the way I have purchased orchard-fresh apples from that moment on.

Start frequenting the orchard early in the season for some quite fine peaches, nectarines, plums, watermelons, and blackberries. The Collinses also have a wide selection of fresh vegetables, but save room in your pantry and refrigerator for the apples. One bite will remind you instantly of how apples are supposed to taste, and you'll find a reason to drive toward their farm every year in the late summer and throughout the fall.

# Cherry Pecan Triangles

### Makes 2½ dozen

½ cup (1 stick) plus 5 tablespoons unsalted butter, softened and divided

½ cup confectioners' sugar

1 egg yolk

1½ cups all-purpose flour

1¼ cups chopped pecans

¾ cup chopped dried cherries

1 cup packed light brown sugar

3 tablespoons heavy whipping cream

3 tablespoons light corn syrup

2 tablespoons sorghum or maple syrup

**These are a favorite of mine to serve around the holidays because the triangles look so festive and taste so good! I dry cherries from the summer in my dehydrator, but many cherry producers sell their fruits already dried, which is a real convenience.**

❧

Preheat the oven to 350°F. Lightly grease a 13 x 9-inch baking dish and set aside.

In the bowl of an electric mixer at medium speed, cream the softened stick of butter (8 tablespoons) and the confectioners' sugar until light and fluffy. Add the egg yolk and mix just until blended. Reduce the mixer speed to low and add the flour, stirring until the mixture is crumbly.

Press the flour mixture on the bottom of the prepared dish. Bake 20 to 25 minutes or until lightly browned. Sprinkle the surface evenly with the pecans and cherries. Set aside to cool. Do not turn off the oven.

Meanwhile, in a saucepan over medium-high heat, combine the brown sugar, remaining butter, cream, corn syrup, and sorghum. Stir constantly until the mixture comes to a boil. Immediately pour over the cherries.

Bake 15 minutes or until golden brown. Cool completely on a wire rack. Cut into squares; then cut in half diagonally to form triangles.

*Mousse* is the French word that means "foam" or "froth." The unflavored gelatin helps fortify and stabilize the mixture while it chills. This tastes like a light, airy pudding, yet it seems richer than a traditional mousse. I like to serve it on warm evenings with crisp sugar cookies for a contrast in texture.

❧

In a microwave-safe bowl, combine the water and gelatin. Let stand 1 minute; then microwave on high power 1 minute. Set aside.

In a mixing bowl, combine the cheese, confectioners' sugar, preserves, and butter. Beat with an electric mixer at medium speed until smooth and creamy. Set aside.

In a separate bowl, beat the cream and sugar until soft peaks form. Beat in the reserved dissolved gelatin until stiff peaks form. Fold into the cheese mixture until well combined. Cover and refrigerate at least 30 minutes. Garnish individual servings with fresh peach slices.

**Note:** If you're using a hand mixer, be sure to clean the beaters between steps.

# Lighter-Than-Air Peach Mousse

**Makes 6 to 8 servings**

3 tablespoons cold water

2 teaspoons unflavored gelatin

1 (8-ounce) package cream cheese, softened

1 cup confectioners' sugar

1/2 cup peach preserves, melted

4 tablespoons unsalted butter, softened

2 cups heavy whipping cream

1 tablespoon sugar

Fresh peach slices for garnish

A nutty toasted oat topping gives this dessert crunch, while the luscious peaches and coconut bubble away underneath. This is a great dessert to place in the oven just before everyone takes their places at the dinner table. It gives everyone time to enjoy the main meal and conversation while it tempts with a tantalizing aroma to remind guests that dessert is on the way!

⤳

Position the rack in the lowest third of the oven and preheat to 325°F. Lightly grease a 13 x 9-inch baking pan and set aside.

Place the oats on a baking sheet and toast 8 minutes, stirring occasionally. Transfer to a mixing bowl and cool completely. Increase the oven temperature to 375°F.

Add the almonds, 1 tablespoon of the flour, the baking powder, and salt to the oats. Set aside.

In a separate mixing bowl, beat the butter and brown sugar with an electric mixer at medium speed until light and fluffy. Add the egg and beat well. Stir in the extract, oat mixture, and coconut. Set aside.

Place the peaches in the prepared dish. Add the remaining flour, sugar, and juice, tossing gently to coat the peaches. Crumble the oat topping over the peaches. Bake until crisp and golden brown, about 30 minutes. Cool at least 10 minutes before serving with a dollop of freshly whipped cream.

# Coconut Peach Crisp

### Makes 6 to 8 servings

1 cup rolled (or old-fashioned) oats

1 cup ground blanched almonds

1 tablespoon plus 2 teaspoons all-purpose flour, divided

1 teaspoon baking powder

1/4 teaspoon salt

2 tablespoons unsalted butter, softened

1/2 cup packed light brown sugar

1 egg

1/8 teaspoon pure almond extract

2/3 cup lightly packed sweetened shredded coconut

2 1/2 pounds peaches, peeled, pitted, and thinly sliced (about 6 large peaches)

1/3 cup sugar

2 teaspoons lemon juice

Whipped cream

# Under the Stars Blackberry Fool

Blackberries hold the honor of being the largest of our wild berries. They are easy to pick because they separate easily from the hull. Blackberries are best used immediately, but if you have to store them, place them in a single layer in the refrigerator. On a clear summer night, serve this dessert outside so you can stargaze and pick out constellations.

❧

**Makes 5¼ cups**

6 cups fresh blackberries
1½ cups sugar
2 tablespoons lemon juice
1½ cups heavy whipping cream

In a large saucepan over medium-low heat, combine the blackberries, sugar, and juice. Cook 6 minutes, stirring until the sugar completely dissolves.

Place half of the blackberry mixture into a blender and puree until smooth. Repeat with the other half. Return the puree to the saucepan and bring to a boil over medium-high heat. Reduce the heat to medium-low and simmer 7 to 8 minutes or until reduced to 3 cups. Stir often to prevent sticking.

Transfer to a mixing bowl. Cover the surface with plastic wrap and refrigerate at least 4 hours. Just before serving, whip the cream to the soft peak stage. Fold into the puree and serve immediately.

I made this one year for a late-spring dinner party when strawberries were just about over for the season. Now it's a tradition! The trick to making perfect meringues is to add the sugar to the beaten egg whites a tablespoon at a time. That's the best way for it to completely dissolve in the egg whites so you don't have a grainy texture.

༈

Combine the brown sugar and water in a large saucepan over medium-high heat. Cook without stirring until the sugar starts to caramelize, about 10 minutes. Swirl the pan to even the brown color.

Add the strawberries and the liqueur. Cook just until the berries are tender, about 3 to 4 minutes. Add the butter and stir until completely melted. Allow to cool and transfer to a lightly greased 8-inch square baking dish.

Preheat the oven to 425°F.

In the bowl of an electric mixer, beat the egg whites at high speed until very foamy. Slowly add the sugar 1 tablespoon at a time. Continue beating until the whites are very shiny and hold stiff peaks, about 5 minutes.

Spread the meringue over the strawberries and bake until golden, about 10 to 12 minutes. Serve warm.

# Caramelized Strawberries with Meringue

**Makes 6 servings**

1 cup packed light brown sugar

2 tablespoons water

3 pints fresh strawberries, capped and halved

2 tablespoons orange liqueur

2 tablespoons unsalted butter

4 egg whites

1 cup sugar

# Sunny Lemon Granite

**Makes 4 servings**

1/2 cup sugar
1 cup water
1/2 cup lemon juice
Fresh mint sprigs for garnish

**Think of this as frozen lemonade!** *Granite* **is the French word for "ice." In Italy, it is** *granita.* **The mixture is stirred frequently while it is in the process of freezing. This give you a granular texture rather than one big frozen chunk. Substitute lime or grapefruit juice for the lemon if you desire.**

∾

Bring the sugar and water to a boil in a medium saucepan over medium-high heat. Boil 5 minutes. Set aside to cool 30 minutes and then add the juice. Stir until well combined.

Pour into a shallow baking dish and place in the freezer. After around 45 minutes the mixture should be frozen about 1 inch around the sides. Use a wooden spoon to stir until it is smooth. Return to the freezer and freeze again. After 45 minutes, beat again. Repeat and then freeze until solid.

When ready to serve, bring to room temperature for 15 minutes. Serve in sorbet glasses with a mint garnish.

**Note:** If you prefer something with a little less pucker, substitute oranges for the lemons.

# Upside-Down Caramelized Nectarines

**This dessert is perfect for when you want to impress your dinner guests but don't want to have something that requires a lot of fuss. The presentation is great, and it's perfect for showing off fresh nectarines. You can substitute fresh apricots or peaches if desired.**

❧

**Makes 8 servings**

1 1/4 cups all-purpose flour

1/2 teaspoon salt

3 tablespoons vegetable shortening

2 tablespoons plus 1/3 cup unsalted butter, divided

5 to 6 tablespoons cold water

1 cup sugar

1/8 teaspoon pure vanilla extract

12 fresh nectarines, pitted, peeled, and halved

In a large mixing bowl, combine the flour and salt. With a pastry blender or two forks, cut in the shortening and 2 tablespoons of the butter until the mixture resembles coarse meal. Add the water and mix just until the dough comes together. Wrap in plastic and refrigerate 5 minutes.

Preheat the oven to 425°F.

Place a 10-inch ovenproof skillet over high heat and stir in the sugar, extract, and the remaining butter. Cook, stirring frequently 5 minutes or until the sugar is golden brown. Place the nectarines cut side down on the caramel mixture and heat 3 minutes.

Meanwhile, on a floured surface, roll the dough into an 11-inch circle. Place over the nectarines and flute slightly. Bake 23 to 25 minutes or until the crust is golden brown.

Cool 7 minutes and invert on a serving platter. Cut into wedges and serve warm.

You'll find lots of plum varieties once you fall in love with this summer fruit. There are dozens of types grown in the South, and all grow in clusters like grapes. This quick recipe is a great way to use plums that are ripening quickly. It comes together in a snap and is a good packer for picnics.

❦

Preheat the oven to 400°F. Lightly grease a 9-inch square baking pan and set aside.

Place the plums in a mixing bowl and toss with 2 tablespoons of the brown sugar. Set aside.

In the bowl of an electric mixer, combine the remaining brown sugar, oats, flour, butter, cinnamon, zest, nutmeg, and baking powder. Blend well.

Place half of the oat mixture in the bottom of the prepared pan, patting down to form a crust. Bake 12 minutes or until brown just around the edges.

Cover evenly with the plum mixture. Crumble the remaining oat mixture over the plums. Bake an additional 20 minutes or until golden brown. Cool completely on a wire rack before cutting into bars. Store leftovers in an airtight container.

# Plum–Centered Picnic Bars

**Makes 15 bars**

1 1/2 cups chopped plums (about 10)

1/3 cup packed light brown sugar, divided

1 1/2 cups rolled (or old-fashioned) oats

1 cup all-purpose flour

12 tablespoons (1 1/2 sticks) unsalted butter, softened

1 teaspoon ground cinnamon

1 teaspoon grated lemon zest

1/2 teaspoon ground nutmeg

1/4 teaspoon baking powder

# Breakfast and Brunch

Fall Fruit Salad

Sunday Sorghum Scones

Applesauce Griddle Cakes

Mushroom Waffles

Lemon Blueberry Pancakes

Citrus Zest Waffles

Wild Mushroom and Bacon Sandwiches

Hot Tomato Grits

Honey-Buzzed Grapes

Cool Summer Melons with Rosemary Syrup

Stuffed Strawberries

Southern Breeze Cantaloupe Limeade

Cornbread Pancakes

Cornbread Waffles

Cornbread Soufflés

Savory Zucchini Pie

Just Peachy Frozen Cocktail

Sugar from the Vine Ice Cubes

Beulah Land Asparagus Pie

Roasted Corn and Lobster Cakes

Mini Strawberry Jam Cakes

Country Baked Eggplant Omelet

Summer Fruit Watermelon Smoothies

Pear Preserves

Winter Pear Pancakes

Blackberry Iced Tea

Farm-Fresh Peach and Chicken Salad

Lady Finger Muffins

Sleepyhead Pumpkin Doughnut Holes

I had this salad at a brunch and fell instantly in love with it, begging for the recipe. When I saw the dressing was a combination of mayonnaise, whipped cream, and sugar, I was shocked. It is marvelous!

❧

In a large serving bowl, combine the persimmons, apples, bananas, and walnuts, stirring gently. In a small bowl, combine the mayonnaise, whipped cream, and sugar, blending well. Pour over the persimmon mixture and toss lightly to evenly coat. Cover and refrigerate at least 1 hour and up to 2 hours before serving.

# Fall Fruit Salad

**Makes 4 servings**

2 ripe persimmons, peeled and sliced

2 cups diced Rome Beauty or Winesap apples, unpeeled

2 bananas, sliced

1/4 cup chopped walnuts, toasted

1/2 cup mayonnaise

1/4 cup heavy whipped cream

1 teaspoon sugar

# Sunday Sorghum Scones

**Makes 6 servings**

3 1/2 cups all-purpose flour
1 cup toasted pecans
1/2 cup packed dark brown sugar
4 teaspoons baking powder
1 teaspoon salt
2/3 cup unsalted butter, slightly softened
1 cup milk
1/2 cup sorghum syrup, divided

**Sorghum syrup is completely different from molasses, even though many cooks get the two confused. Sorghum is made with only sorghum cane. Molasses can be a blend of any number of different sugarcanes. Sorghum is much better, and I always have it in my pantry. So grab the Sunday newspaper and hit the deck. These incredible scones only need a cup of hot coffee or a glass of ice-cold milk.**

Preheat the oven to 425°F. Lightly grease a baking sheet and set aside.

In a mixing bowl, combine the flour, pecans, sugar, baking powder, and salt. With a pastry blender or 2 knives, cut in the butter until the mixture resembles coarse meal.

In a small bowl, combine the milk and 1/3 cup of the sorghum syrup. Add to the flour mixture and mix lightly with a fork until it forms a soft dough. Turn out onto a lightly floured surface and knead 6 times. Divide the dough in half. Roll each half into a 7-inch round. Cut each round into 8 wedges. Place on the prepared baking sheet and pierce the tops with a fork. Brush the tops with the remaining syrup. Bake 16 to 18 minutes or until golden brown. Serve warm.

Most apple orchards have a great selection of apple products for sale. You can find everything from fried pies to cider to jellies. Select one of their jars of applesauce for this recipe, either plain or flavored. If flavored, consider omitting the ground cinnamon.

# Applesauce Griddle Cakes

**Makes 6 to 8 servings**

2 cups biscuit mix

1 cup milk

1 cup applesauce

2 eggs, lightly beaten

1/4 teaspoon ground cinnamon

Lightly grease a griddle or skillet and place over medium-high heat.

Meanwhile, in a mixing bowl, stir together the biscuit mix, milk, applesauce, eggs, and cinnamon, blending until smooth.

Using a 1/4 cup measure cup, pour the batter on the griddle. Cook until the tops are covered with bubbles and the edges look dry, about 2 minutes. Flip and cook until golden brown, about 1 minute longer. Repeat with the remaining batter. Serve warm with pure maple syrup.

Take brunch to another level with these savory topped waffles. Making something out of nothing sure does taste good. Be sure to use a nice mix of mushroom varieties, rather than one kind, for more interest.

# Mushroom Waffles

**Makes 8 servings**

1 recipe Cornbread Waffles (page 250)

3 tablespoons unsalted butter

12 ounces assorted mushrooms, sliced

1 1/2 teaspoons chopped fresh thyme

1/4 teaspoon garlic salt

1/8 teaspoon black pepper

Prepare the Cornbread Waffles according to the recipe.

Melt the butter in a large skillet over medium-high heat. As soon as it begins to foam, add the mushrooms and thyme. Sauté 8 to 10 minutes or until browned. Season with the salt and pepper. Cover and refrigerate to use later or cool slightly for immediate use. If chilled, gently warm before using.

Preheat the oven to 400°F. Cut the waffles into wedges and place on an ungreased baking sheet. Heat 2 minutes, turn over, and heat 2 minutes longer. Mound the mushroom mixture on each wedge. Serve immediately.

## Oakview Farms Granary

Joe and Patty Lambrecht
164 Dewberry Trail
Wetumpka, Alabama 36093
(334) 567-9221
E-mail: oakview164@aol.com
Website: www.oakviewfarms.com
Consumer Experience: General store, farm market

Sitting on the scenic southern foothills of the Appalachian Mountains is Wetumpka, Alabama, a fun city to let roll off your tongue. While passing through on a trip to Montgomery, Alabama, I discovered Oakview Farms Granary, owned and operated by Joe and Patty Lambrecht. Now it's a destination, and every single time I go, I load up on farm-fresh eggs.

If you've never had a fresh egg, you don't know what you're missing. The difference in taste could rightfully be compared to a winter tomato versus one just pulled from the vine. The fresh difference is evident in the velvety texture, the color of the yolk (influenced by feed), and the flavor.

Joe and Patty actually began their business as a Saturday sideline where they concentrated on grinding grains, and I truly love their stone-ground yellow cornmeal. When they both retired, Oakview Farms Granary became their full-time passion for showcasing organically and hydroponically produced foods. It quickly expanded to include chickens, eggs, goats, blueberries, peppers, tomatoes, lettuce, and honey.

The entire family is a part of the farm business, including their daughter, Kelly, and granddaughter, Kristen, who is in charge of the petting zoo. Stop by for those fantastic brown eggs weekly, and pick up everything else while you are there on Thursday mornings, or on Fridays and Saturdays year-round.

You'll notice the light texture of these pancakes, and the credit goes to beaten egg whites and club soda in the batter. Be sure to invest in a bottle of blueberry syrup for this recipe. You'll be glad you did!

❧

Lightly grease a griddle or skillet and place over medium-high heat.

Meanwhile, in the bowl of an electric mixer, beat the egg whites on high speed until stiff peaks form. Set aside.

In a separate bowl, combine the flour, sugar, baking powder, and salt. Make a well in the center. Add the egg yolk, club soda, milk, zest, extract, and oil, mixing well. Fold in the egg whites and blueberries and gently combine.

Using a 1/4 cup measuring cup, pour the batter on the griddle. Cook until the tops are covered with bubbles and the edges look dry, about 2 minutes. Flip and cook until golden brown, about 1 minute longer. Repeat with the remaining batter. Serve warm with blueberry syrup.

**Note:** You can substitute orange or lime zest for the lemon, if desired, but change the extract to vanilla.

# Lemon Blueberry Pancakes

**Makes 6 servings**

2 egg whites

1/2 cup all-purpose flour

3 tablespoons sugar

3 teaspoons baking powder

1/4 teaspoon salt

1 egg yolk

1/2 cup club soda

1/4 cup milk

2 tablespoons grated lemon zest

1 teaspoon pure lemon extract

1 tablespoon canola oil

1 cup fresh blueberries

Blueberry syrup

### Fruitville Grove Farm Fresh Market

Skim Elmenani
7410 Fruitville Road
Sarasota, Florida 34240
(941) 377-0896
E-mail: fruitvillegrove@aol.com
Website: www.fruitvillegrove.com
Consumer Experience: Farm market, purchase online

When you think of Florida, it doesn't take long for citrus fruits to come to mind. Sun-filled oranges, lemons, limes, tangerines, and grapefruits are evidence of South Florida's tropical weather and are in abundance constantly. I make a stop at Fruitville Grove Farm Fresh Market anytime I'm even remotely close to Sarasota.

Their honeybell, or minneola, grabbed me years ago, and as hard as I try, I can't seem to get my fill of them.

A minneola, one of two varieties of the tangelo, is a cross between a grapefruit and a tangerine, and quite frankly, it is a great marriage. It may look small in comparison to oranges, but it is literally packed with juicy sweetness. I love that the skin is easy to peel and juice oozes from every part. It is a high-demand fruit, and I know why. It's simply delicious, and as soon as the season hits, I'm there.

But this family farm is known for more than their honeybells. It is a year-round, one-stop shopping place when you want to get everything you need and move on. They have loads of fresh produce that is harvested daily, so pick up all you need of peppers, tomatoes, eggplant, and peaches. And don't skip out before you swing through the Grove Market. They have a huge selection of cheeses, salsas, and barbecue sauces, as well as small-batch-produced Amish canned goods that are one of a kind.

A side trip to Fruitville Grove will do exactly what your Florida vacation was designed to do . . . make you slow down for a moment, stretch your legs, and enjoy the fruits of the Florida harvest.

Wake up sleepy taste buds with these zingy waffles. These are nice served with just whipped cream or a smear of butter. Any leftovers can be frozen for later use when breakfast needs to be on the go. Just pop the frozen waffle in your toaster . . . no need to thaw first.

# Citrus Zest Waffles

**Makes 5 to 6 servings**

2 cups all-purpose flour

1/2 cup sugar

2 teaspoons baking powder

1/2 teaspoon baking soda

1/4 teaspoon salt

3 eggs, separated

1 1/2 cups buttermilk

6 tablespoons fresh orange, lemon, or lime juice

4 tablespoons unsalted butter

2 tablespoons grated orange, lemon, or lime zest

Lightly grease and preheat a waffle iron.

In a large bowl, combine the flour, sugar, baking powder, baking soda, and salt. Make a well in the center and set aside.

In a separate bowl, whisk together the egg yolks, buttermilk, juice, butter, and zest. Add to the flour mixture, stirring to combine.

In the bowl of an electric mixer, beat the egg whites until soft peaks form. Gently fold into the batter. Pour 1/2 to 3/4 cup of batter on the hot iron. Cook until golden brown. Repeat with the remaining batter. Serve warm with pure maple syrup.

I use the name "wild" loosely here, because even those mushrooms labeled as such are cultivated. The more variety you have with the mushrooms, the better this dish will be. It's perfect for late risers who have missed breakfast and can't wait until lunch. Brunch to the rescue!

Place the bacon in a large sauté pan over medium heat and cook until crispy. Drain on paper towels and set aside. When cool enough to handle, break the bacon into coarse pieces.

Add the oil to the pan with the bacon drippings. Add the onions and garlic and sauté 1 minute. Add the mushrooms and sauté 2 minutes or until they start to soften. Stir in the wine and marjoram and cook until just about dry, around 10 minutes. Season with the salt and pepper.

Split the rolls and place a slice of Swiss cheese on each half. Evenly distribute the mushroom mixture on the bottom half of the rolls. Sprinkle with the reserved bacon and top with the other roll half. Serve warm or at room temperature.

# Wild Mushroom and Bacon Sandwiches

**Makes 8 servings**

8 slices bacon, cut in large squares

2 teaspoons olive oil

2 green onions, chopped

3 garlic cloves, peeled and chopped

5 cups sliced wild mushrooms

1 cup dry red wine

1 teaspoon chopped fresh marjoram or thyme

1/4 teaspoon kosher salt

1/4 teaspoon black pepper

8 yeast rolls

8 slices Swiss cheese, cut in half

# Hot Tomato Grits

This is the perfect brunch recipe and a savory addition for all those sweet muffins, jams, and crepes. It can be stirred while the final details of the brunch are being taken care of, then placed on the table hot. There will be no leftovers.

❧

**Makes 6 servings**

2 bacon slices, chopped
1 (28-ounce) container low sodium chicken stock
1 cup quick-cooking grits
2 large tomatoes, peeled and chopped
2 tablespoons chopped green chiles
1 cup shredded Cheddar cheese

Place the bacon in a heavy saucepan over medium heat. When the bacon is crisp, gradually add the stock. Bring to a boil.

Stir in the grits, tomatoes, and chiles. Return to a boil, stirring frequently. Reduce the heat to low and simmer 15 to 20 minutes, stirring frequently. Add the cheese, cover, and remove from the heat source. Stir after 5 minutes and serve hot.

# Honey-Buzzed Grapes

This is such an easy recipe to make, and it gets raves every time I serve it. The ice-cold grapes are especially nice served during the hot summer months. I like to serve them with fancy cocktail picks during brunch on the patio.

❧

**Makes 6 servings**

1 pound seedless green grapes
1 teaspoon fresh lemon juice
2 tablespoons port
1/4 cup honey

Wash and stem the grapes, placing them on paper towels to dry.

In a small bowl, mix together the juice, port, and honey. Place the grapes in a single layer in a shallow container. Pour the glaze over the grapes, cover, and refrigerate at least 4 hours. Remove from the refrigerator 20 minutes before serving. Spoon any excess juices over the grapes.

### Beachaven Vineyards and Winery

Ed and Louisa Cooke
1100 Dunlop Lane
Clarksville, Tennessee 37040
(931) 645-8867
E-mail: thefolks@beachavenwinery.com
Website: www.beachavenwinery.com
Consumer Experience: Tour, purchase on site,
purchase in retail outlets

When I moved to Tennessee in 1989, Beachaven Winery was the first agriculture-based business I visited. I have been a rabid fan of theirs ever since and consider Ed and Louisa Cooke two of my dearest friends.

Drive along I-24 toward the southern Kentucky line and there is it: a drop-dead-gorgeous vineyard and winery that you can see from your vehicle. You will immediately find a way to exit the interstate in order to arrive there, and since the winery is open year-round, stop by anytime you are in the area. The vineyard rows seem to pull you in and wrap you in welcoming, "Come sit for a spell" arms.

Their grapes are absolutely breathtaking, and I always feel transported to some far-away land when I stand among the vines. Pencil-straight rows of American native grapes, such as Catawba and Sunbelt (a Concord twin), drip with juice-filled fruit, along with French hybrids, such as Seyval Blanc, that have proven to be stable in Tennessee's up-and-down climate.

Louisa's father, Judge William O. Beach, was a true pioneer of the Tennessee wine industry and seamlessly passed the love on to his only daughter. His son-in-law, Ed, has meticulously woven that same passion into their grapevines. The evidence is showcased through more than 500 regional, national, and international awards rightfully adorning their exquisite wines.

The tour, which includes the famous champagne celler, is an educational look into how grapes become wine. And you'll get to see plenty of their harvest to taste and see how they measure sugar inside. You'll also get to see how this versatile fruit goes from being picked to being bottled.

While there are always plenty of worries—like weather, birds, deer, and numerous other farming calamities that loom within the season—there is also a calm that covers the vineyard. Louisa told me the best part of growing grapes is their beauty, the quietness of being in the fields with them, the peace you feel, and the pride you experience when the fruit from a nice growing season is harvested. Well said, Louisa, and I couldn't agree more. Cheers to the finest way to drink local fruit!

# Cool Summer Melons with Rosemary Syrup

You cannot believe how delicious this syrup makes even ordinary, not-quite-in-season melons taste. Whole peppercorns may seem a little strange to have in this recipe, but they become the secret ingredient that you'll taste but not be able to pinpoint.

❧

**Makes 4 servings**

1/2 cup water

1/2 cup dry white wine

1/2 cup sugar

2 (1 1/2-inch strips) orange zest

1 1/2 teaspoons chopped fresh rosemary

1 teaspoon black peppercorns

1 (5-pound) honeydew or cantaloupe, or half of each

1/4 cup fresh orange juice

In a medium saucepan over medium-high heat, bring the water, wine, sugar, zest, rosemary, and peppercorns to a boil. Stir until the sugar dissolves, reduce the heat to low, and simmer 4 minutes, stirring occasionally.

Strain the mixture through a fine mesh sieve into a bowl, pressing to remove as much moisture as possible from the solids. Discard the solids. Refrigerate 30 minutes.

Meanwhile, cut the melon into wedges or balls and arrange them in a shallow serving bowl. Stir the orange juice into the syrup. Gently toss the melons with the syrup. Cover and let stand at room temperature 1 hour. Toss again and serve.

# Stuffed Strawberries

I served these delicacies at my friend Michelle's baby shower, which she missed because she was having the baby! She still hears about the yummies she missed on her son's birthday! It's a great spring brunch addition that you'll love.

❧

**Makes 18 strawberries**

20 large fresh strawberries, divided

4 ounces cream cheese, softened

2 tablespoons finely ground walnuts or pecans

4 tablespoons confectioners' sugar

2 teaspoons orange liqueur

Finely mince two strawberries and set aside. Cut a thin slice from the stem end of each remaining berry to form a base. Starting at the pointed end, cut each strawberry into four wedges, cutting to but not through the stem end. Set aside.

Beat the cream cheese with an electric mixer at medium speed until fluffy. Stir in the minced strawberries, ground nuts, sugar, and liqueur. Transfer to a pastry bag with no tip or gallon-size zip-top bag with the bottom corner snipped. Pipe about 1 teaspoon into the center of each strawberry. Refrigerate up to 2 hours before serving.

### Bush–N–Vine Farm

Bob Hall
1650 Filbert Highway
York, South Carolina 29745
(803) 684-2732
E-mail: info@bushnvinefarm.com
Website: www.bushnvinefarm.com
Consumer Experience: Produce stand,
spring and fall festivals

Melons . . . I can't make it through the summer without them. They beg to be eaten out of doors and ice-cold no matter whether you've picked a watermelon or a cantaloupe. I'm always on a search for the finest.

At first glance, the produce stand at Bush-N-Vine Farm is not very impressive. It's an aged barn that has the farm name painted on the old tin roof. There are cutouts for windows, but there is no glass. It looks weathered and worn and just like something a farmer would sell out of. But I remind myself that I'm not looking to buy a building. I'm looking for a great summer melon.

Bush-N-Vine Farm has been in business since 1979, and I dearly love the melons they pile inside that building that now looks different and sports loads of character. Starting in mid-July, those ripe sugar melons begin to be pulled from the vines and transported to the sales area. I am practically standing there waiting as they arrive.

For the longest time, I didn't think I liked cantaloupe. But one plucked from the plant and cut right there in the field changed my thinking. Now I realize that I just hadn't had one that was completely ripe, which is why I depend on farms like Bush-N-Vine to harvest them at the exact time when it's perfect. And they do!

While you are there, you can fill your arms with lots of other farm-fresh items, but just make sure you've already made room for the melons. And as you pull away and see the stand in your rearview mirror, it will make you smile at how wrong your first impression was!

# Southern Breeze Cantaloupe Limeade

**Makes about 5 cups**

1 whole cantaloupe, peeled, seeded,
and cut into chunks

1 cup water

1/2 teaspoon grated lime zest

1/2 cup sugar

1/4 cup fresh lime juice

Fresh lime slices for garnish

**If you want to really kick up the breeze for adults, mix this concoction with champagne, white rum, gin, or vodka! Then your Sunday brunch will be especially memorable.**

Place the cantaloupe, water, and zest in a blender and process until smooth, stopping to scrape down the sides. Pour through a wire-mesh strainer into a pitcher, pressing the pulp with the back of a wooden spoon. Discard the pulp.

Stir in the sugar and lime juice until the sugar dissolves. Serve over ice and garnish with lime slices.

# Cornbread Pancakes

These thin, pliable creations can be used as a brunch crepe. They are terrific to wrap around chicken, beef, mushroom, or cheese fillings.

≈

Place the cornmeal, flour, buttermilk, oil, eggs, and salt in a blender and process until smooth. Refrigerate 1 hour.

Lightly grease a small skillet and place over medium heat. Pour 1/4 cup of the batter into the hot skillet, tilting to make sure the batter covers the entire bottom of the skillet. Cook 3 minutes or until the top is set. Cool on waxed paper and repeat with the remaining batter.

### Makes 8 servings

3/4 cup plain cornmeal
3/4 cup all-purpose flour
2 1/2 cups buttermilk
1/4 cup vegetable oil
4 eggs
1 teaspoon salt

# Cornbread Waffles

All waffles are not the same and this one is perfect when you want something out of the ordinary. It makes a great anchor for savory toppings or can be cut in wedges and served with hot soups or stews. With just a bit of preparation, you've got a scratch-made novelty with little effort.

≈

Place the cornmeal, flour, buttermilk, oil, eggs, and salt in a blender and process until smooth. Refrigerate 1 hour.

Preheat the waffle iron; then pour 1/2 cup of the batter into the hot iron. Cook until golden brown. Repeat with the remaining batter.

### Makes 8 servings

3/4 cup plain cornmeal
3/4 cup self-rising flour
1 1/2 cups buttermilk
1/4 cup vegetable oil
3 eggs
1 teaspoon salt

You'll love the uniqueness of these individual portions that instantly make your guests feel special. Have the rest of your food items prepared and ready to serve as soon as these lovelies come out of the oven.

❧

Preheat the oven to 350°F. Lightly grease six (6-ounce) soufflé or custard cups and set aside.

In a mixing bowl, combine the cornmeal, baking soda, and salt. In a separate bowl, whisk together the yogurt, corn, egg, milk, and oil. Add it to the cornmeal mixture, stirring just until moistened. Spoon evenly into the prepared cups.

Bake 30 minutes or until a knife inserted in the center comes out clean. Serve immediately.

# Cornbread Soufflés

## Makes 6 servings

1 cup plain cornmeal

1/2 teaspoon baking soda

1/2 teaspoon salt

1 (8-ounce) carton plain yogurt

1 cup creamed sweet corn

1 egg

1/4 cup evaporated milk

2 tablespoons vegetable oil

No need to worry about a crust with this pie. It forms its own, which means this is a quick company dish that can go from brunch to dinner. The zucchini can be shredded ahead of time to make stirring it together simple.

❧

Preheat the oven to 350°F. Lightly grease a 9-inch pie plate and set aside.

In a mixing bowl, combine the zucchini, eggs, onions, baking mix, cheese, oil, salt, pepper, sage, and paprika. Blend well. Transfer to the prepared pie plate.

Bake 45 minutes or until a tester inserted in the center comes out clean. Cool 10 minutes on a wire rack before slicing and serving.

# Savory Zucchini Pie

**Makes 8 servings**

2 cups shredded zucchini

2 eggs, lightly beaten

1 white onion, peeled and chopped

3/4 cup all-purpose baking mix

3/4 cup shredded sharp Cheddar cheese

1/4 cup vegetable oil

1/2 teaspoon salt

1/4 teaspoon black pepper

1/4 teaspoon dried sage

1/4 teaspoon paprika

# Just Peachy Frozen Cocktail

**What did we do before blenders were invented? You can substitute vodka or light rum for the gin in this adults-only beverage.**

❧

**Makes 4 servings**

3 large peaches, peeled, pitted, and sliced

1 tablespoon lemon juice

2 tablespoons sugar

$1/4$ teaspoon pure almond extract

$1/4$ cup gin

1 cup crushed ice

1 (1-liter) bottle sparkling water, club soda, or ginger ale

Fresh mint sprigs

Place the peaches, juice, sugar, extract, gin, and ice in a blender and process until smooth. Add the sparkling water just before serving with a garnish of mint.

# Sugar from the Vine Ice Cubes

**These cubes are delicious in lemonade or can turn an ordinary glass of tea into a charming refresher. It's a great use for extra watermelon you have that is taking up room in your refrigerator.**

❧

**Makes 12 cubes**

$1/2$ medium seedless watermelon, cut into cubes

2 tablespoons lemon juice

Place the watermelon in the container of a food processor or blender. Add the juice and process until smooth. Pour through a fine mesh strainer into a pitcher or container with a spout. Discard any solids.

Pour the mixture into ice cube trays and freeze. When frozen, transfer to a freezer container, label, and seal. Or enjoy immediately with your favorite beverage.

This pie could easily make you believe heaven is on earth. It is a perfect mixture of crisp fresh asparagus, cheese, eggs, and flaky pie crust. I usually serve it for brunch, but it's also great when you want breakfast for dinner. Remember to select asparagus spears that are close to the same thickness for even cooking.

❧

Bring a large saucepan of water to a boil. Add the asparagus and cook 30 seconds. Drain and plunge in ice water for 30 seconds. Drain and coarsely chop when cool enough to handle. Set aside.

Preheat the oven to 425°F. Place the pastry in a 10-inch tart pan. Prick the bottom of the pastry and place the tart pan on a baking sheet. Bake 10 minutes. Set aside to cool on a wire rack. Reduce the oven temperature to 375°F.

Meanwhile, melt the butter in a medium skillet over medium-high heat. As soon as it begins to foam, add the onions and sauté 5 minutes or until tender. Set aside.

Brush the bottom and sides of the crust with the mustard. Sprinkle with half of the cheese, asparagus, onions, and then top with the remaining cheese. In a mixing bowl, whisk together the half-and-half, eggs, salt, and pepper. Pour over the cheese.

Bake 25 minutes or until set and golden brown. Let stand at least 10 minutes before slicing and serving warm.

# Beulah Land Asparagus Pie

**Makes 8 servings**

1 1/2 pounds fresh asparagus, trimmed

1 Single-Crust Pie Pastry (page 191)

1 tablespoon unsalted butter

1 sweet onion, peeled and diced

2 tablespoons Dijon mustard

1 cup shredded Monterey Jack cheese, divided

1 1/2 cups half-and-half

2 eggs

1/4 teaspoon salt

1/4 teaspoon black pepper

Sunday brunch has never been as elaborate or elegant as it will become when these treats are served. A nice, sweet chili sauce makes a great dip for the cakes. You must serve these with champagne.

∽

Preheat the oven to 400°F.

In a medium bowl, toss the corn with 2 tablespoons of the canola oil, 1/2 teaspoon of the salt, and 1/4 teaspoon of the pepper. Arrange in a single layer on a jelly-roll pan. Roast 18 to 20 minutes or until the kernels are golden brown. Set aside to cool, then transfer to a mixing bowl.

Place the clam juice in a small saucepan over medium-high heat. Cook 20 minutes or until the liquid has reduced to 1 tablespoon.

Meanwhile, heat the beer in a separate small saucepan to 110°F. Add the yeast to the beer, stirring well to combine. Set aside to cool 5 minutes.

To the corn bowl, stir in the remaining canola oil, salt, and pepper. Add the reduced juice, yeast mixture, milk, flour, butter, hot sauce, and lobster, mixing well. Cover and let rise in a warm place, free from drafts, 30 minutes.

Meanwhile, pour the oil to a depth of 3 inches in a Dutch oven and bring to 350°F. Beat the egg whites with an electic mixer at medium speed until stiff peaks form. Fold into the yeast mixture. Carefully drop tablespoons of the batter into the hot oil. Do not crowd the pan. Fry 2 minutes or until golden brown. Repeat with the remaining batter. Serve warm.

# Roasted Corn and Lobster Cakes

**Makes 10 servings**

2 cups whole kernel sweet corn

3 tablespoons canola oil, divided

1 teaspoon salt, divided

1/2 teaspoon white pepper, divided

1 (8-ounce) bottle clam juice

1/3 cup dark beer

3/4 teaspoon active dry yeast

1/2 cup milk

1 cup all-purpose flour

2 tablespoons unsalted butter

2 tablespoons hot sauce

1 cup finely chopped cooked lobster

Vegetable oil

3 egg whites

# Mini Strawberry Jam Cakes

These delicious jam cakes will transform your Mother's Day brunch, and you can use fresh strawberry jam made from the season's harvest. Actually, I first made these jam cakes to show off some nontraditional lunchbox treats. But who can resist them until lunch? You can also serve them as a dessert, or better yet, before church on Sunday morning.

### Makes 6 cakes

1/2 cup (1 stick) unsalted butter, softened

3/4 cup sugar

1 teaspoon finely grated orange zest

2 eggs, separated

1 1/2 cups all-purpose flour

1/2 teaspoon baking powder

1/4 teaspoon salt

1/4 cup milk

6 tablespoons strawberry jam

1 1/2 cups confectioners' sugar

1/4 cup fresh orange juice

Preheat the oven to 350°F. Grease or line a muffin pan with paper liners and set aside.

In a medium mixing bowl, beat the butter, sugar, and orange zest with an electric mixer at medium speed until light and fluffy. Add the egg yolks one at a time, beating until creamy. Set aside.

In a small bowl, sift together the flour, baking powder, and salt. Beginning and ending with the flour mixture, alternately add the flour and milk to the butter mixture. Set aside.

In the bowl of an electric mixer, beat the egg whites to soft peaks. Gently fold into the batter. Divide half the batter evenly among the muffin cups. Make an indentation in the middle of each and fill with 1 tablespoon of the jam. Top with the remaining batter.

Bake 28 to 30 minutes. Unmold the cakes and transfer to a wire rack to cool. In a small bowl, whisk together the confectioners' sugar and juice. Place the wire rack over parchment paper and drizzle the cakes with the glaze.

## Ponchatoula High School

Alice Dubois
19452 Highway 22 East
Ponchatoula, Louisiana 70454
(985) 351-5149
Website: www.tangisschools.org/schools/phs
Consumer Experience: School sales

Ponchatoula was a sleepy Louisiana town for quite some time. Then Robert Cloud introduced his Klondike strawberry variety, and for more than 40 years, it was practically the only strawberry suited to grow in the Louisiana climate.

Fast-forward to 2005 and strawberries take on an even more dramatic role. After Hurricane Katrina hit, Alice Dubois at Ponchatoula High School noticed that a lot of special-needs kids were being mainstreamed into agriculture classes. Instead of throwing up her arms in frustration, she decided to give those students a true agricultural experience.

They began by making dog treats for rescued service dogs. Alice noticed that integrating measuring, pouring, and counting made for a perfect exercise for these students. That led to a school garden of vegetables, like broccoli, turnips, spinach, lettuce, kale, and green onions. Now it has grown into strawberry production, and anyone around the area will testify as to how in-demand they are in this community.

As a further lesson in giving, any excess is donated to their local food bank. Yes, the strawberry is the king of all berries, and the students of Ponchatoula High School prove it every spring with their luscious "school-grown" fruit.

If you think omelets are rubbery and forgettable, you have to give this recipe a try. It's like no other omelet you've ever had, thanks to the pan-roasted eggplant. Don't limit it only to breakfast meals. It's equally delicious for a late Sunday dinner.

෴

Place the oil in a large ovenproof skillet over medium-high heat. Add the eggplant and sauté 3 minutes or until tender. Stir in the peppers.

In the bowl of an electric mixer, beat the eggs, milk, salt, and pepper. Pour into the skillet. As the mixture begins to cook, lift the edges with a spatula and tilt the pan so the uncooked portion flows underneath. Reduce the heat to low and cover. Cook 10 to 12 minutes.

Meanwhile, preheat the broiler. Sprinkle the egg mixture evenly with the cheese and place under the broiler. Broil 2 minutes or until the edges are golden brown. Scatter the chives over the top and cut into wedges. Serve immediately.

# Country Baked Eggplant Omelet

**Makes 6 servings**

3 tablespoons olive oil

2 cups peeled and chopped eggplant

1 (12-ounce) jar roasted red peppers, drained and chopped

10 eggs

1/2 cup milk

1 teaspoon salt

1/2 teaspoon black pepper

2 tablespoons grated Parmesan cheese

1 tablespoon chopped fresh chives

# Summer Fruit Watermelon Smoothies

I made this concoction with some leftover watermelon from a cookout one year, and now it's a lazy summer morning regular. It's incredibly quick. If you want, add light rum or vodka just before serving your adult friends.

In a blender or food processor, combine the watermelon, ice, sherbet, and lime juice. Puree 30 seconds or until smooth. Pour into chilled glasses and serve immediately.

**Note:** Excess can be poured into ice cube trays and frozen for later use in your favorite beverages or to keep this smoothie ice-cold through your commute to work.

## Makes 4 servings

3 1/2 cups cubed seedless watermelon
1 cup crushed ice
1 cup raspberry sherbet
1 1/2 tablespoons fresh lime juice

My grandmother used to make the best pear preserves in the whole world. I still crave them and use this recipe every year to make a batch. No matter how much I make, it never seems to make it to the next year. Hot biscuits seem to gobble it up!

❧

In a large Dutch oven, combine 1 1/2 cups of the sugar with the water. Place over medium-high heat and cook rapidly 2 minutes. Add the pears and boil gently for 15 minutes. Add the remaining sugar, stirring until the sugar dissolves.

Cook about 25 minutes or until the fruit is clear. Cover and let stand 12 to 24 hours in the refrigerator.

Heat the fruit and syrup to boiling. Pack the fruit into hot canning jars, leaving 1/4 inch headspace. Cook the syrup 3 to 5 minutes longer if too thin. Pour the hot syrup over the fruit. Wipe the jar rims and adjust the lids. Process 5 minutes in a boiling water bath. Cool completely on wire racks away from drafts.

# Pear Preserves

**Makes 5 half-pints**

3 cups sugar, divided
2 1/2 cups water
6 to 7 pears, peeled, cored, and sliced

Serve these pancakes to guests who visit in the fall and around the holidays, when fresh pears are flooding the market. Unlike most fruits, pears actually improve in flavor and texture after they are harvested. Store them at room temperature until ripe and only refrigerate the ripe ones you can't use immediately.

❧

Lightly grease and preheat a griddle or skillet over medium-high heat.

Meanwhile, in a large bowl, combine the flour, baking soda, sugar, cinnamon, and salt. Make a well in the center and add the buttermilk, eggs, and butter. Stir just until moistened. Gently fold in the pears.

Pour the batter by 1/4 cupfuls onto the griddle. Cook until the tops are covered with bubbles and the edges look dry, about 2 minutes. Flip and cook until golden brown, about 1 minute longer. Repeat with the remaining batter. Serve warm with pure maple syrup.

# Winter Pear Pancakes

**Makes 4 to 6 servings**

2 cups all-purpose flour
1 teaspoon baking soda
1/4 teaspoon sugar
1/4 teaspoon ground cinnamon
1/4 teaspoon salt
2 cups buttermilk
2 eggs
2 tablespoons unsalted butter, melted
1 large pear, cored, peeled, and chopped

# Blackberry Iced Tea

**Makes 7 ½ cups**

3 cups fresh or frozen blackberries
(if frozen, thaw)
1 ¼ cups sugar
1 tablespoon chopped fresh mint
8 regular-sized tea bags
4 cups boiling water
2 ½ cups cold water
Fresh mint sprigs for garnish

**This is a quite lovely version of Southern fruit tea that utilizes either fresh or frozen berries; so take your pick. If you have extra of this recipe on hand, pour the excess into ice cube trays and freeze. Use the next time you prepare this recipe and the cubes will not dilute the fruit tea as they melt.**

In a mixing bowl, combine the blackberries and sugar. Use the back of a wooden spoon to crush the berries. Add the chopped mint and set aside.

Place the tea bags in a large pitcher. Pour the boiling water over the tea bags. Cover and let steep 5 minutes. Remove the tea bags and squeeze out the excess moisture. Discard the tea bags.

Pour the tea over the blackberry mixture. Let stand at room temperature 1 hour. Strain into a pitcher through a fine-meshed sieve, and discard the solids.

Add the cold water and stir well to blend. Cover and refrigerate until ready to serve over ice.

### Barber Berry Farm

Ken and Anida Barber
2362 Alabama River Parkway
Millbrook, Alabama 36054
(334) 549-4710
E-mail: kenandanida@barberberryfarm.com
Website: www.barberberryfarm.com
Consumer Experience: Pick your own, farm market,
local delivery

Blackberry cobbler is by far my favorite cobbler of all time. It begs to be served warm from the oven and to be crowned with a scoop of homemade vanilla ice cream. For that reason, I will rise very early in the morning, douse myself with bug spray, and head to the picking grounds of this most perishable fruit. It is necessary for me to go through this ritual in order to have that mind-blowing cobbler.

Ken and Anida Barber feel the same way about blackberry cobbler, but their crop is in their own backyard. After successful careers in the Air Force, this spunky couple decided to try their hands at farming. After studying hard and seeking much guidance, they discovered they are really good at it! The result is 35 (300-foot) rows of six different kinds of blackberries that beg to be picked each summer. They also grow blueberries, muscadines, scuppernongs, peaches, plumcots, nectarines, persimmons, plums, pomegranates, pumpkins, and hydroponic strawberries and tomatoes.

Many people just don't like the south Alabama heat in the summer, so Barber Berry Farm booths can be found at the Millbrook and Auburn farmers' markets with loads of pre-picked fruit. That's makes it easy to run by on your way home from work and have that cobbler ready for an evening feast on the front porch.

**Brunch just took a fruity twist. One day, I had no seedless grapes for my chicken salad, so I substituted fresh peaches instead. Now I regularly forget to buy the grapes on purpose! Only fresh peaches will work in this recipe.**

⁓

In a large bowl, combine the chicken, celery, onions, peaches, and pecans. Mix gently. In a separate bowl, combine the mayonnaise, sour cream, salt, and pepper. Gently toss with the chicken mixture. Cover and refrigerate at least 2 hours before serving.

To serve, scoop the salad onto lettuce leaves that are placed on chilled plates. Garnish with the parsley.

# Farm-Fresh Peach and Chicken Salad

**Makes 6 servings**

2$^1$/$_2$ cups chicken, cooked and cubed

2 celery stalks, diced

$^1$/$_2$ cup diced red onions

1 large fresh peach, peeled, pitted, and cubed

$^1$/$_2$ cup chopped pecans, toasted

$^1$/$_2$ cup mayonnaise

$^1$/$_2$ cup sour cream

$^1$/$_2$ teaspoon seasoned salt

$^1$/$_2$ teaspoon black pepper

Lettuce leaves

Fresh parsley sprigs for garnish

## Cotton Hills Farm

Jeff and Carol Wilson
2633 Lowrys Highway
Chester, South Carolina 29706
(803) 581-4545
E-mail: thewilsons@cottonhillsfarm.com
Website: www.cottonhillsfarm.com
Consumer Experience: Tour, pick your own,
farm stand, purchase online

*I*t's ironic that one of my favorite places to purchase armloads of okra is at a farm named Cotton Hills. Perhaps that's because okra and cotton are in the same botanical family and are close relatives. And that you can pick cotton and okra at the same time is a bonus activity that many have never experienced.

Jeff and Carol Wilson are four generations removed from Theodosia Abell Wilson, who was given the farm as a wedding gift back in the 1800s. The original cotton farm has now been transformed into a tremendous fresh vegetable destination to anyone traveling even close to Chester, South Carolina.

The Wilsons have more than 80 acres just in produce, but it's the okra that I crave and must purchase by the cooler-full. Perhaps it's the South Carolina soil, or maybe it's because I know it comes from their own fields that turns me in their direction during the hottest of the summer months. But I love the fact that the okra is never overly large and is beautifully uniform for all of the canning and freezing plans I have for it.

Try to resist picking just a few boles of cotton while you are there . . . it is impossible! Then gather plenty of their other vegetables that are equally fresh and homegrown. They have everything from tomatoes and corn to peppers and onions. Once everything is loaded into coolers in my car, I like to end the experience with a scoop of their totally refreshing lemon ice cream in a sugar cone. Now, that's how you shop for okra!

One of the sweetest nicknames for okra is "lady fingers" because supposedly, ages ago, someone thought they resembled each other. I love to serve these okra-filled muffins with country ham and grits. The key to muffin success is to slice the okra very thin.

*Lady Finger Muffins*

Makes 1½ dozen

2 cups self-rising cornmeal

1 teaspoon sugar

1/2 teaspoon salt

1/4 teaspoon white pepper

1 1/4 cups milk

2 eggs, lightly beaten

1/4 cup vegetable oil

1 teaspoon Worcestershire sauce

1/4 teaspoon hot sauce

2 cups thinly sliced okra

1/4 cup chopped onions

Preheat the oven to 400°F. Lightly grease muffin pans and place in the oven while it is preheating. (Use a cast iron muffin pan if available.)

Meanwhile, in a mixing bowl, combine the cornmeal, sugar, salt, and pepper. Make a well in the center and set aside.

In a separate bowl, combine the milk, eggs, oil, Worcestershire, and hot sauce. Add to the dry ingredients, stirring just until moistened. Fold in the okra and onions.

Spoon the batter evenly into the prepared cups, filling each no more than two-thirds full. Bake 20 minutes or until lightly browned. Remove from the pans immediately and serve hot with butter.

# Sleepyhead Pumpkin Doughnut Holes

**Makes 18 doughnut holes**

Canola oil

1/2 cup plus 1/3 cup sugar, divided

1 teaspoon plus 1/4 teaspoon ground cinnamon, divided

1 1/2 cups all-purpose flour

1 tablespoon baking powder

1/2 teaspoon salt

1/4 teaspoon ground ginger

1/4 teaspoon ground nutmeg

1 egg, lightly beaten

1/2 cup cooked, mashed pumpkin

1/4 cup milk

2 tablespoons vegetable oil

1/2 teaspoon pure vanilla or walnut extract

**Having trouble getting certain family members to rise and shine? Here's your new secret weapon for accomplishing the task. These doughnut holes will get them rolling right out of bed and racing to the kitchen! It's a great way to use pumpkins from your visit to the local pumpkin patch.**

Pour the oil to a depth of 2 inches in a Dutch oven and place over medium-high heat. Bring to 375°F.

Meanwhile in a small bowl, combine 1/2 cup of the sugar with 1 teaspoon of the cinnamon. Set aside.

In a medium mixing bowl, combine the remaining sugar and cinnamon with the flour, baking powder, salt, ginger, and nutmeg. Make a well in the center and set aside.

In a separate bowl, combine the egg, pumpkin, milk, vegetable oil, and extract. Blend well and add to the flour mixture. Stir just until moistened.

Carefully drop tablespoons of the batter into the hot oil. Fry until golden brown, around 4 minutes, turning once to evenly brown. Drain on paper towels and while hot, roll in the reserved cinnamon sugar. Serve warm.

# Canning Instructions

*H*ome canning is never a time to experiment away from U.S. Department of Agriculture–approved recommendations. There are only two safe methods: a boiling water bath and a pressure canner. You will change between the two depending on what you are canning.

## Boiling Water Bath Canning

The boiling water canning method is where the jars are simply covered with boiling water and heated for a certain amount of time. It is safe for any high-acid foods, such as tomatoes, fruits, pickles, jams, jellies, marmalades, and preserves. It works because the heat level from boiling water is sufficient to destroy microorganisms that cause foods to spoil.

A water bath canner is a very large covered pot with a rack in the bottom. It must be deep enough to cover the jars with at least 1 inch of boiling water. The diameter should be no wider than 4 inches past your stove's burner.

The rack in the bottom prevents the jars from touching the bottom and allows hot water to freely move beneath the jars. I like racks with dividers so the jars will not touch each other or fall over during the canning process.

## Pressure Canning

Canning under pressure is the only way to safely can vegetables other than tomatoes. Although it is not done as frequently, it is also the method for canning meats, poultry, and seafood. Because pressure canners take foods to a higher temperature than the boiling point of water, they prevent food spoilage in all low-acid foods.

Pressure canners can have either a dial or a weighted gauge that tells you how much pressure is building up inside the pot. They also have a rack in the bottom and an extremely tight-fitting lid that prevents steam from escaping while you are canning. Follow the manufacturer's directions carefully, and read all of the instructions before beginning the process.

# Equipment

**Mason-type jars**—use only those specifically designed for home canning
**Two-piece canning lids**—do not use old porcelain-lined zinc lids or glass caps
**Jar funnel**—designed just for home canning purposes and keeps the mess at bay
**Bubble wand**—removes air bubbles from the jar before the lid is added
**Lid wand**—has a magnet on the end to help remove canning lids from hot water
**Kitchen timer**—to signal that the processing time is over
**Jar lifter**—very necessary for taking the hot jars out of the canner

# Processing

No matter which method you are using to can, certain rules apply that must be followed. First, make sure you keep the canning jars and lids hot from the beginning. This prevents any possible breakage when the jars are filled with hot food. I use the dishwasher to clean the jars, then to keep them warm until I need to get them filled.

Headspace is the amount of space in the jar between the top of the food and the bottom of the lid. This amount of space will vary according to the food you are canning. Too much headspace can result in the jar not sealing properly. Too little headspace could cause the food to spill out during processing, resulting in a jar that doesn't seal. Always follow whatever headspace you are instructed to have in your recipe.

When filling the hot jars with food, air bubbles can become trapped inside. During processing, these rise to the top of the jar, and suddenly you have too much headspace. Use a bubble wand to eliminate this problem. Simply run the flat wand down the side of the jar to release the bubbles after filling. Then you are ready to seal the jar.

Wipe the rims of the jar with a damp, clean towel before placing the lid and screwband onto the jar. Any small particles of food on the rim can prevent an airtight seal. After processing, there is no need to tighten the screwband any further.

In the canner, make sure you keep the jars upright at all times. Any tilting of the jars can cause the food within to spill into the sealing area around the two-piece lid.

Each food has its own processing time, and it will vary according to the density of the food, the liquid it is packed in, and the pH of the food. Overprocessing gives you overcooked food while underprocessing can give you spoiled food. Do not guess at the processing time. Use a kitchen timer, and if you momentarily leave the kitchen, take it with you.

After removing the jars with a lifter from the canner, place them right side up directly onto a wire cooling rack. Leave at least one inch of space between each of the jars for proper cooling. Make sure the cooling area is away from any drafts from heating or cooling vents. Leave the jars undisturbed for 24 hours.

As the jars cool, you will hear a popping sound. After 24 hours, test the seal by pressing your finger in the center of the lid, which should be concave. It should not move. If it is not sealed and moves when pressed, refrigerate the food and use within 2 or 3 days. Store sealed jars in a cool, dry, dark place until ready to use.

# Acknowledgments

What a total joy it has been to research and write this cookbook. It feels like a part of me that has been waiting patiently to come forth for decades. I have so many to thank for pushing me forward and pulling me back.

Bryan Curtis is a man like no other I have ever known. He is so much more than a cherished friend. He has been my teacher, my guidebook, my idea stretcher, my word counselor, and my recipe inspiration. I am eternally grateful to have him in my life and in the role of my cookbook brother. I owe him more than I could ever repay.

Heather Skelton at Thomas Nelson is like a dream come true. She has been fluid, encouraging, and has allowed me the freedom to do what I love. What a joy it is to know there are people like her in this world of ours.

Ron Manville and Teresa Blackburn are nothing short of remarkable. Working with them is like being with food and photography artists. Their talent inspires me and I adore them both and love them like siblings.

To my exceptional friends who have endured the process of taste testing recipe after recipe, I honor you! What a privilege it is to have such an incredible support system surrounding me. Thank you for your gentle suggestions of recipe tweaks and changes as well as your thunderous applause at the end results.

My husband, George, will forever be the love of my life. He has encouraged me, believed in me, and has never lost his contagious zest for all things agriculture. It humbles me that I have been gifted with such an incredible man. God has certainly been very good to me.

# Index